TAINTED

The JaRon Eames Story

JKE PRODUCTIONS
New York City

TAINTED

Published by: JKE Productions
New York, New York
Email: jaroneames@gmail.com

JaRon Eames, Publisher / Editorial Director
Yvonne Rose/QualityPress.Info, Production Coordinator

ALL RIGHTS RESERVED No part of this book may be reproduced or transmitted in any form or by any means – electronic or mechanical, including photocopying, recording or by any information storage and retrieved system without written permission from JaRon K. Eames. The publication is designed to provide accurate and authoritative information in regard to the subject matter covered. It is sold with the understanding that the Publisher is not engaged in rendering legal or other professional services. If legal advice or other expert assistance is required, the services of a competent professional person should be sought.

© Copyright 2019 by JaRon Eames

ISBN: 978-1-0878-49782
Library of Congress Control Number: 2019919643

Printed in the United States of America

Dedication

To my Wonderful Parents,
Cookie and Louis L. Eames, Sr.

Contents

Dedication v

Contents vii

Chapter 1: The Beginning 1

Chapter 2: The 1960s 12

Chapter 3: The 1970s 57

Chapter 4: The 1980s: *The End of Drinking Was Close* 103

Chapter 5: The Nightmare Starts 154

About the Author 210

Acknowledgements 212

Recordings 214

Chapter 1

The Beginning

The date was December 21st, 1953. The town was Baton Rouge, LA. It was 10:01 A.M. to be exact when I made my entrance onto the world stage. I have no knowledge of my first thoughts of course, however, I'd be willing to bet whatever you have, that it had something to do with 'Show Business.' What wonderful memories I have to this day of growing up in a place and time surrounded by love, laughter, good music, the best foods, and a family that was as good as it got as far as I'm concerned. And at the start of this book, March 30th, 2007, we are all still best friends and enjoy each other's company a great deal. (It's now 2019 and I'm finishing the book, because I had more to say, more life to live, and it's in Gods time when I finish this.)

Being the youngest of six kids, five boys and one girl, I wasn't aware of it, but it was brought to my attention on more than a few occasions, that I was spoiled as they say rotten. It never bothered me, and personally, I found it to be a rather pleasant way to have grown up. But what is Spoiled?

Webster defines it as among other things, to pamper excessively. I prefer to just call it what it was, loved. And when children are truly loved, as my brothers and sister and I were, it carries us through life with decency and humanity for others. I believe, lacking in those who didn't have or experience a deep and true love as kids. I'm not judging. We all have to play the cards we are dealt with.

The Eames Family - 1953

"A man who has been the indisputable favorite of his mother keeps for life the feeling of a conqueror; that feeling of success which often induces real success."

- ***Sigmund Freud***

This was said about Frank Sinatra, but then he was an only child of his mother Dolly. In my case, it just may be that it happens to fall on the youngest for some reason. I'm sure all of us were loved equally but the last child seems to be the spoiled one. As far back as I can remember there were always parties in my parents' home. My father

The Beginning

was one of the most remarkable men God ever put breath in. My mother too, for that matter. He came up the hard way in the deep South. Born in 1920, growing up in Louisiana, (I'm sure you can figure out how it was during that time in the American south for people of African Ancestry). He worked odd jobs as a kid to survive, selling peanuts, fruit, and newspapers, which is what many kids did in those days, and should do today. He graduated from **McKinley High** in 1939.

IN THE 1950'S JARON'S FATHER, WAS THE FIRST BLACK MAN TO GET A MASTERS DEGREE IN BUSINESS FROM LOUISIANA STATE UNIVERSITY, BATON ROUGE, LA

My father graduating from LSU in Business.

He received his College Degree from Southern University in 1947 and went on to become the first member of his race to get a Master's in Business from all-White Louisiana State University, LSU. In the late 40s and early 50s, he owned several businesses, trying to make a go of it. He had a consultant and accountant service, the Eames E-cono-washateria, worked in the Southern University auditors' office, in extended services and was the editor of the local black paper, The Capitol City Press. He taught accounting in the school of business at Southern University, until he resigned in 1956 to become one of the founding members and managing officers of the newly chartered First Federal Savings and Loan Association in Baton Rouge, Louisiana. All of this, I might add, was accomplished in a time when virulent racism was as blatant as daylight. But as Maya Angelou says, "And Still I Rise".

Some members- board of Dir. @ First Federal- B.V.Baranco, L.L.Eames, Leo S.Butler Mrs.G. L. Netterville, and Mrs. F. G. Clark

It was at First Federal that my father Louis L. Eames Sr. forged a national reputation as an administrator, executive officer, and community leader, as he skillfully managed the growth and stability of the savings and loan association. Under his tenure, the financial institution became one of the most highly regarded successful minority associations in the country (the 7th largest Black Savings and Loan). He served as managing officer and executive vice president for 30 years, during which time he was cited innumerable times for his excellent abilities in the field of high finance and accounting. He was widely appreciated for his knowledge and assistance in making available the necessary funding for countless numbers of black families to acquire and build homes. During his years at First Federal, housing for black families throughout Baton Rouge and surrounding areas improved, allowing for better neighborhoods in which to live. My father is listed in Who's Who Among Black Americans, and also listed in the Directory of United States Banking Executives. He held memberships in numerous civic and social organizations, among which are the Baton Rouge chapter of Kappa Alpha Psi fraternity, and the Alpha Xi Boule of Sigma Pi Phi Fraternity. Also, he was a 32nd degree Mason. Most important, he was my best friend.

My parents at one of their parties in the 1950's

My mother, who could pass for Lena Horne's sister, worked at Southern University in the communication switchboard office. At that time, we had a tiny two-story home, which I was really too small to remember. I only remember the large split-level home that was about 3,000 Sq. Ft. We moved into that home when I was four years old in 1957. It was a lovely suburbia community, all middle and upper-middle-class black family homes. There's a plaque now at the entrance of Southern Heights saying it's the oldest black neighborhood of brick homes.

Most, if not all the kids in my neighborhood went to a semi-private black segregated school. Southern University Laboratory School, a 1-12th grade school that was located on the campus of Southern

University. Before I was old enough for school, I used to go with my father every day to his office and play until my mother got off work and picked me up. Being the youngest of six kids, all of my brothers and my sister were already in school. My father would take my mother to work and the kids to school, and he and I would go to this small green wooden bank on Harding Blvd. All of these places are a five to ten-minute drive from our home.

The Eames Family home built 1956

One morning, everybody was getting ready for work/school, having breakfast. Afterward, they all piled in the car. *(Can you imagine, a house with 6 kids running all over the place?) I'd go mad.*

I had been sick the night before and my parents decided to let me sleep and father would drop them all off at school and come right back for me, this would take all of about 10-15 minutes.

So, wouldn't you know it, as soon as they pulled out of the driveway I jumped out of bed, looked out the window and watched my family drive away? I'm all of four years old and I'm watching my wonderful family leave me. In a very real sense, I was 'home alone 'long before Macaulay Culkin. I went into panic mode. I jumped out of bed in my PJ's and flew out of the door barefoot chasing the car and screaming to the top of my little lungs, to no avail. I went to the neighbor's house, Alice Washington, she had left for work and nobody was home. (her beautiful daughter Maryella who lived there after Alice died, was burned to death along with her husband and cats due to a major fire in 2018). Shocking, I was in Baton Rouge recently and it's now just a big empty lot. I ran to another neighbor, Mildred Higgins.

She had gone to work and taken Aeneid and Rodney to school; I ran yet to another neighbor. No one was home. The neighborhood was being built from the ground up as they say, and at the time there were only a few houses and lots of open lands.

I now was in a state of complete and utter shock at all of four years old. I preceded to run to the main highway to get to my mother's office. (I call it a main highway, but in reality it's a narrow two-lane street, Harding Blvd). Which, now that I think of it was past my father's office. I guess I didn't see the car at his office since they had just left. Ummm. Anyway, I preceded to cross this major highway all two small lanes of it, and a car stopped, recognized me and picked me up. She was the librarian at the high school. She was of course in a dither as to why I was half-naked running down the highway; but I couldn't speak, only cry. She took me to my mother's office, who was, upon seeing her baby without shoes and in PJ's and now hearing how this nice lady found me running down the street, was truly beside herself as I'm sure you can imagine.

She asked me over and over what had happened, and then she figured out that I had seen the family leave me and was coming to her, but not a word came out of my mouth. I couldn't speak. The shock was too much. When I did speak again I had a severe stutter, which I had all through my teenage years, young adult years, and even today, but today I have managed to almost alleviate that problem. Except certain words and numbers on the phone.

Oh, by the way, the nice lady who picked me up on the highway was Mrs. Deborah Fisher. In 2005 she was trapped in her home (along with her 80-year-old sister) whose body was found floating in her New Orleans home after Hurricane Katrina. Ms. Fisher died shortly afterward.

I started first grade; I was 5. Ms. Mcleod was my teacher from 1st. - 3rd grades. She was a wonderfully stern woman. It was a very good school Black teachers who really cared and helped nurture Black children. I really liked my teacher, and she didn't take any BS.

The school is still producing productive students, as I write.

It was a large school, great scenery, weeping willows, and heavy hanging moss. Grade 4-6 was equally fun as were the teachers who did a great job with us. But I think by that time I'd had enough of school and was ready to move on to something else. I still remember most of all, Friday's lunch, because in the school cafeteria we had a breaded fish dish and the softest rolls. I can still taste them. But I was getting pretty sick of school…

Upon entering Junior high I had become increasingly bored. When I was about 6 -8 years old my parents' friends would say to me, as all parents friends say to kids, what do you want to be when you grow up? And I'd say with the greatest of pride, "A banker like my daddy". Then, one day when I was about 9-10 years old one of my parent's friends asked me, (everybody in my hometown while growing up called me by my middle name which is Kanard, they still do) Kanard, what do you want to be when you grow up, and I looked that woman right in the eye and said a' **Movie Star'**.

Well, I'll have you know that person looked at me like I had two heads and hurried off to do whatever she was doing before I upset the apple cart with my foolishness. Little did we both know that from that day forward I set out on my journey. I have, over time come to realize that this is my birthright. My divine birthright. From time to time in this book, I will quote from the wonderful teachings from an **Indian sage:**

Paramahansa Yogananda's 'The Law of Success'

> *"The Lord created me in his image. I will seek him first, and make sure of my actual contact with him. Then, if it's his will, may all things - wisdom, abundance, health - be added as part of my divine birthright."*

The only star that I ever heard people talk about at that time out of Baton Rouge was Donna Douglas who played Ellie May Clampett on the CBS hit **'The Beverly Hillbillies'** which ran from 1962-1971. (Now in 2019 we have a version of Jed Clampett in the white house with Jeftro Bodine and Ellie May) So, my saying I wanted to be a movie star was unheard of. But I knew I wanted something to do with showbusiness. To this day I have no idea where it came from. Or what it meant to be a Star. Perhaps, just going through life with a 'glow'.

I began to dread school. I learned to dislike school at an early age (not due to the teachers, they were simply great, and did a wonderful job with us, or the students). But since I'm an honest person and want my first book to reflect that honesty, I have to say I hated school. (I call this my first book, because it was, my story was in my book Jazz Conversations. It was unedited and only a manuscript when it was published, simply awful. The book was printed without my consent. It didn't belong in a jazz history book, so now I'm writing it to stand alone.) I'm still trying to get it removed from the internet after all these years. I had a deep dislike for school. It wasn't school as much as the structure of it all. I'm just not made for that. I knew it at an early age. I needed to fly, to soar…

It just wasn't for me. I felt like a Krispy Kreme doughnut without the icing. There were so many more exciting things I wanted to be doing. Because I had a stutter I didn't like to read out loud in class, because all the kids laughed. (we are still friends to this day, all of my childhood friends: Jonathan W, Walter B, Kennard W, Carl S, Mada. M, Gloria, Kathy S, Kathy D, in fact we all stay in touch and we celebrated out 50th high school reunion in 2001.) When the teacher called on me to read I made an effort, but soon just stopped.

It really was very funny though; my head would twist around trying to get the words out and my face and /mouth would become contorted. ca ca ca ca can I go to the th th the bathroom. But I soon put a stop to the laughter, I learned to laugh first and loudest. But after a while I just tuned out, not because I stuttered, that never bothered me or stopped me from doing anything I wanted to do. Remember Aunt Clara who stuttered? She was from the 1964' **Bewitched** ' sitcom TV show. I loved her so much. She was the first person I ever saw on TV who stuttered. It was the funniest thing to me.

I just didn't care about being there. I prayed to get out of high school ASAP.

Chapter 2

The 1960s

We had a Black radio station in my town of Baton Rouge, Louisiana. It was WXOK, and the host was a character named Diggy Doo. He played the best R&B ever. It was called 'race' music in those days. (How I long for the days of 'race' music-) Otis Redding, Jackie Wilson- Sam Cooke, Al Green, Major Lance, Marvin Gaye, Motown, BB King, Muddy Waters, Etta James, Jazz, blues, 50s harmony groups, etc.) In fact, in some ways I long for the days of segregation.

For one thing, the music was better, it wasn't full of self-hate and anti-black lyrics, and hatred of Black women and unnecessary violence as we find in the popular Black culture today. And what's profoundly sad, it's Black folks who are producing this madness, and consuming it. However, it is my understanding that those who really 'control' Hip Hop community, those who really 'pull the strings' on what gets played and what succeeds, has told some of these ghetto kids 'you must talk about your women, call each other N____, and be as vile and biased, as you can, and we will make you rich'.

James Baldwin said, 'The Black performer is still in the battle with the white man's image of Blacks, which the white man, clings to in order not to be forced to revise his image of himself'.

The original Hip-Hop was positive with a message of enlightenment to the masses.

The wonderfully profound 'Last Poets' who taught through their politically-charged raps, slick rhythms, with their goal to raise African-American consciousness; and many say it was one of the direct links to what became Hip-Hop today. But that was coming from a place of Black consciousness and shockingly positive.

According to the fascinating Dick Gregory who was a good friend of Michael Jackson, the Jackson family, and many others, believe that's one of the reasons many think Michael was assisted in his demise by forces who didn't want his true love and positive political messages to come through in his music. And because of his astute business acumen, due to his 'control as a free agent' and his Sony catalog There are very dangerous and powerful forces out there. So, one must be careful.

Today, there are those who seem to have this need for a return of minstrels. As Malcolm said, (we are often dealing with people who are Masters of Tricknology). But the Blacks in the industry with 'clout' who should have known better did nothing to stop it because I guess they want to be hip and young, and not make waves. Or, maybe they were 'powerless' to do so.

Or perhaps, they just wanted to get paid? There's more money in the muck. I'm just asking. Many have sold their souls to Satan for the green paper.

But have you looked into their eyes? Empty. I had that chance, which you will read about later in this book.

For many years mostly what one saw on BET from the 90s was negative images of themselves through hip-hop Videos. **'Black**

Entertainment Television'. How sad is that those deep feelings of hopelessness and inadequateness are played out and overcompensated by thug behavior. Today, in my opinion, we have lost an entire generation of black youth, if not two, to this self-hate mindset. Just turn on the news in any city and Blacks are killing Blacks in sagging pants at an alarming rate. Young girls are getting pregnant and there's no male figure to help her bring up the child and growing up listening to music calling them dogs and animals and other vile names by young black males just adds to this culture of self-hatred. Now they will loudly proclaim, but we are getting paid. Wow!

However, it seems to me that many of our Black youth today are hated, feared, dismissed, and despised around the country, even as the White's (who are the largest purchasers of hip-hop), and Asians mimic the Hip Hop genre. Could it be that it's more money to be made to imprison the young inner-city youth today than it does to put them through school?

Human Rights and political organizations have asked if it's a new form of slavery. Over 2 million Blacks and Hispanics are in jails across America working for a pittance. And they are fighting and killing and hating each other while the powers that be sit back and watch the 'divide and conquer' strategy play itself out. Instead of hating and fighting each other; and instead of fighting over some street corner turf which neither owns. Blacks and Browns should be uniting and joining forces and resources to make a real difference. But oppression makes one do foolish things. (remember Martha Reeves and the Vandellas signing " Love makes me do Foolish Things"1967?)

The Prison industrial complex is big business, and some of its investors are on Wall Street…

They are building prisons daily and they plan to fill them. The trap has been set. Many in the Black community point to the 1980s when a report came out of direct involvement of the CIA in introducing Crack Cocaine into the ghettos across America, which destroyed untold thousands of lives. Of course, the major newspapers and the US Government denied any involvement in this. But I believe they also denied any involvement in the Tuskegee Syphilis Experiment, where 399 poor and impoverished African American sharecroppers from Macon County Alabama - many with syphilis - were used as 'test subjects.' The year was 1932 when it started... By 1947 penicillin was an effective cure for the disease, but these Black men were **never** treated and for 40 years they were studied to see the effects of this dreaded illness. They passed it on to their girlfriends, boyfriends, wives and newborn babies. The researchers wanted to observe the full and long-term effects of syphilis. Many suffered. Many died. This is pure evil…

It continued until 1972 when it was leaked and terminated. The Tuskegee Syphilis Study was cited as '**arguably the most infamous biomedical research in US history'**.

Perhaps this is just one reason among many why Blacks see things which affect us differently than others may view it. Now, of course, AIDS is being questioned.

The 42nd President of the United States, Bill Clinton, issued a formal apology in 1997 saying in part, "I am sorry that your federal government orchestrated a study so clearly racist." Thank you, Mr. President. That's a start.

If you flood the inner cities with vile, negative, poisonous music, violent video games, bad schools, the worst teachers, drugs, no jobs, single mothers, no fathers, racist cops, hormones in fast food fed to inner-city youth, cheap malt liquor with high alcohol content, etc. Well, you can see why they keep building prisons and not schools. But where are the parent's today? That's where it starts…in the home.

I'm just asking. The ruin of a nation begins in the homes of its people. But what I have just described is the very visible minority of Black youth.

The majority of Black kids are in schools, with two parents in the house, many are going to college, planning wonderful things, doing great things, working towards the American dream, but you don't hear about those, because it doesn't sell papers, and knocks down the myth of all 'young Blacks are criminals.. You rarely hear about the Promise Academy Charter Schools, or the Urban Prep Academies and all of the black graduates from college. When the young Black male has been demonized and cast off so thoroughly, that when he is killed by a police officer in a 'questionable situation', the first thing the public says is, "oh he must have done it."

That's a very dangerous mindset. A new paradigm needs to take place in the Black communities nationwide, and in America.

Time is running out.

That said, the Hip Hop era has made many **Black millionaires**. Now I can be wrong, but I think it's the first time a 'Black creative art's genre' has produced real trust fund babies in numbers. That's a good thing. But was the damage that it did to the Black masses worth it? To produce a handful of wealthy Blacks?

James Allen, in his book 'As A Man Thinketh', urges us to cherish our vision, cherish our ideals, cherish the music that stirs in our heart, the beauty that forms in our minds, for out of these visions will grow all delightful conditions.

In other words, dream lofty dreams, because, as you dream, so shall you become."

Say Amen, Somebody!

When James Brown shouted **' Um, wit yo bad self, Say It Loud'** in **1969** or Marvin Gaye asked **'What's Going On'** in **1972**, when groups like the Temptations, and Miracles, the Four Tops, the Spinners, Drifters, among others sang about love, hope, dreams, ambitions, Martha Reeves was **'Dancing In The Streets'**, Curtis Mayfield, encouraged us to **'Keep On Pushing'** Sam Cooke, was sure **'A Change Is Going To Come'**"& Aretha screamed **'R-e -s-p-e-c-t '** it made everybody feel good. It brought us together as a nation in general and people of color together, in particular. (Maybe that's why Black music changed and went negative because the powers that be had an agenda to promote the worst in Black culture, as opposed to the best. I'm Just asking. But those of us of a certain age, you remember that period of music. Think about it. Am I right?

Maybe it was just the time. I sure miss them. Growing up in Baton Rouge 50s- 60s in Jim Crow, I would go weekly to the movies.

The Ann, Lincoln, the Temple, and the Cook theaters, owned managed by James Cook and Fred Williams, respectively.

There were Black soulful nightclubs, with real soul music on the jukebox. We had restaurants, Ethel's Kitchen and Delpit's Chicken Shack, both of which are still there. Two of the few. They were small black places, but ours.

I'm happy to say, I remember small stores, motels, insurance companies, contractors, gardeners, a real self-contained community. If we couldn't get what we needed as people, from the US Government, we had to get it from ourselves. We couldn't go downtown and shop in most, if any, White stores because of Jim Crow/segregation, so we as a community had to spend our dollars with each other and many flourished. As political activist Bob Law says in his wonderful book, **'Voices for The Future** ' The thriving businesses of the 30s' 40s, 50s did not exist so much out of self-reliance as did out of self-defense. Blacks had no choice; it was do for self or do without'. He relates a brilliant story to illustrate his point as told to him by Terri Williams author of 'The Personal Touch" when she said, **'Every morning In Africa, a Gazelle wakes up and knows that it must outrun the fastest cheetah, or it will be killed. Every morning the Cheetah wakes up and knows it must outrun the slowest Gazelle, or it will starve to death. It doesn't make any difference if you are the Cheetah or the Gazelle. When the sun comes up you'd better start running**.

During this period, Blacks were really pulling ourselves up by our bootstrap despite church bombings, lynchings, being jailed and beaten for the most part, just because whites could… I can't help but think of the great poet Maya Angelou when she said, **"And Still I Rise"**.

Then what happened next was a wickedly clever idea. Integration. Which of course had its good parts on many levels. Some weren't so good. Blacks could go to White theaters, stay in White hotels, eat-in White restaurants, shop in White stores, and they (Blacks) ran in droves spending all of their hard-earned dollars, and White business thrived. Blacks were deliriously happy sitting in White establishments, after centuries of separate public existing, while the Black areas which were once rich with culture, and community support disintegrated. Because of the Jim Crow laws, my parents and all Blacks had to stay at Black-owned establishments. One was the Marsalis Motel owned by Jazz pianist Ellis Marsalis father, which opened in 1943 outside of New Orleans.

Many Black leaders including Martin L. King, Adam C. Powell, Justice Thurgood Marshall stayed there. However, the irony is that the Civil Rights achievements and integration opened up the White Hotels, and businesses; and Blacks walked, no ran to them and over time many black-owned establishments closed. Marsalis Motel went out of business and was sold in 1986. I could be wrong, but what I believe really happened in America at that time was desegregation, not integration. A good friend of mine, playwright and author Calvin A. Ramsey wrote a children's book called, "Ruth and the Green Book", about blacks traveling through the Jim Crow south.

While we spent our money in the white business, the idea on the other side, for the most part, spending white dollars in Black business, wasn't there.

When I go home today, the area where I grew up has changed. It's a shell of what it was when I was growing up, in some respects. That was in the 1960s. Of course, there are some wonderful things going on now after many years of neglect, but I do see growth. Many areas around the country today, because of a changing mindset and a large black middle, upper-middle class, and wealthy Blacks, positive things are happening, and we are starting to see a rebirth of communities. (Perhaps I'm remembering through rose-colored glasses) However, I'm happy to say that nationwide, the Black community is making a much stronger resurgence. However, many business owners are from other countries. Sad to say, many come here and adapt the ways of the oppressors.

In the 1960s, I was a complete and utter fool for R&B, I knew all the songs, and heard them all day and night. Instead of learning reading writing and arithmetic I was listening day and night to my little transistor radio that we had to hold to our ear. I don't think I knew or listened to any white music, except for the Righteous Brothers, and I thought they were Black, as everybody else did until we saw them on Ed Sullivan TV show. How funny is that? There were some country singers I heard on the radio, which I liked, but didn't know anything about them. My love of 'White singers' came later when I discovered that wonderful sound of Frankie Avalon, Frankie Valli, Patty page, Elvis, Ricky Nelson and two of my favorites Bobby Darin and Sinatra.

I saw many singers on late night Hollywood movies singing in films like the lovely and very talented Doris Day, (I didn't know any of their names,) the Doo Wop/ harmony groups, and so much more. I fell madly in love with it. But then, when I heard the White singer's cover versions of the Black originals like Elvis singing Big Mama Thornton's **"Hound Dog"** or Pat Boone singing Little Richard's **"Tutti Frutti"** and Fats Domino's **"Ain't That A Shame"** or even Peggy Lee's big hit **"Fever"** when you hear the original version by one of my favorite singers Little Willie John, it's an entirely different experience. However, the White versions got the airplay and sold off the charts while the Black originals never got the push or airplay to compete, unfortunately; and unless one is into the history of the music they may never know these facts. Little Willie John Fever did very well, I might add. But the song, even to this day, is associated with Peggy Lee.

One of my quirks is getting to the source. For instance, very few people today even talk about the fact that the world-famous '**Cotton Club'** Featuring the biggest Black acts in American music, Armstrong, Ellington, Cab Calloway, Lena Horne, and the greatest dancers in my opinion ever, Harold and Fayard Nicholas –known as the Nicholas brothers, could perform; yet the club didn't allow blacks in the audience. But which is not common knowledge was that it was originally owned by the Black World heavyweight boxing champ Jack Johnson in 1920.(It was then called the Club Delux) That is until 1923 when the Prohibition Gangster from Leeds England Owney Madden and his mob decided he 'wanted' it and made it into a 'Whites only' club called the 'Cotton Club.' During that time Harlem was all white, mostly Irish and Germans. Madden was also part owner of the Stork Club, one of the most famous of society hangouts, and a fight promoter.

My parents at The Kappa Alpha Psi (Black & White ball) 1960's, 2nd brother Carl, Eldest Brother Louis Jr.

My parents, sister and me in NYC 1964. New York Hilton

The year was 1964. My parents brought my sister and me to New York. We were staying at the New York Hilton on 6th Ave and 54th St. I was beside myself with glee. I was 11 years old; my sister was 14. In New York, one should stay in a high-rise Hotel to get the (full effect) view and the ambiance of the city. We ordered room service and looked out over the great city of New York. *We had only one tall building in Baton Rouge, the Louisiana state capitol. Conceived by Governor Huey P. Long, it was finished in 1932, and 34 stories. (The Governor was also assassinated there in 1935.)* We were way up high in the Hilton. I don't remember the floor now, but we could see as far as China. Across the street was/is the Warwick Hotel.

One day I heard all of this commotion down on the Street. There were what seems to my 11-year-old eyes thousands of people outside screaming and crying, holding up signs, and just going mad. (Now I come from a small sleepy southern town where this was unheard of,) so I felt compelled to explore. I asked my father if I could go downstairs to see what was going on. He said no. That was not the answer I wanted; I assure you. So, a short time later I asked again and begged. Oh, how I carried on.

He said OK but stay in the lobby. I ran to the elevator, went to the lobby, and walked myself out onto the streets. Well, I found out by going right outside big as day, that The Beatles had just arrived in America, for the first time ever, and were staying right across the street at the Warwick Hotel. It was February 7, 1964. The Beatles were in New York to make their debut on the famous Ed Sullivan Show, which is right around the corner from the Hotel and where the David Letterman Show taped from. The Ed Sullivan Show was as big as it gets. It ran from June 20, 1948 to June 6, 1971.

Remember I had no idea who the Beatles were; in fact, nobody in America, (outside of New York) did at that time. My taste in music was Motown, James Brown, Little Stevie Wonder (and I might add that if you didn't see James Brown in the 1960s, you missed one of the seven wonders of the world. There was nothing like him and there will never be), also Little Anthony, Gladys Knight, Wilson Pickett, etc. However, the mob out in the street surely knew who the Beatles were. I had never witnessed anything like it. In Baton Rouge, Louisiana, after dark, one could, as we say, 'hear a fly piss on cotton' It's so quiet. I was paralyzed with excitement, by such drama and energy, the sheer madness of it all. It was life in the big city. I returned to the room unimpressed by the Beatles, but most impressed by the scene they caused, so much so that I looked my father in the eye, reported what I had seen and why all of the commotion was going on outside.

But most importantly, I told him 'when I turn 19, I'm moving to New York City'. He patted me on my head and said, OK son, now go to bed. Well, just for the record I'll have you the reader know that I kept my word; and at 19, I was living in New York City on East 85th Street where I still live today. It was December 1972 when I moved to New York. (but more about this later) In fact, *All About It*. Oh, by the way, a few years later, I could sing every song the Beatles recorded and loved them, as the world came to love them.

Earlier in this book, I mentioned "The Law of Success". I find such comfort in these words.

> *"Your success in life does not altogether depend on ability and training, it also depends on your determination to grasp the opportunities that are presented to you.*
>
> *Opportunities in life come by creation, not by chance.*
>
> *You, yourself, either now or in the past (including the past or former lives) have created all opportunities that arise in your path. Since you have earned them, use them to the best advantage."*
>
> **-Paramahansa Yogananda**

Back in Baton Rouge, I couldn't wait to get out of high school, I was an uninterested student. I had fights, physical and verbal. In fact, the only time I got a whipping by my father was when after many times of getting put out of school for fighting or some other disruption, my father said "son if I have to leave my job and come to your school one more time and see the teachers I'm 'gonna beat the shit out of you'."

In those days, parents could still beat some sense into us. Another thing kids lack today. A good old fashion beating. Well wouldn't you know it, my father got the call from the principal that I had been fighting again. He came to pick me up from school. We were inside our lovely large split-level home (in the mid-60s, house and garden came to do a layout of our home for the magazine) and I'm sitting at the kitchen table on a high bar stool. My father was going on and on, about he'd had it, and was tired of leaving his work for my foolishness, and he was pissed. Well, I made the mistake of saying something smart. (Now my father had a real temper, which is where I get mine from, and I have prayed to God for years to help me maintain it because I do go off.) After my smart and unwise comment, he slapped me so hard I flew off the bar stool and landed on the floor.

I was too outdone; I mean completely and unequivocally outdone in the most real sense. I couldn't believe what had just happened. Besides Being speechless. He screamed, go to your room. I didn't speak to him for days. One reason as I look back on a life that I had so many fights in school was that I was a pretty boy. I believe that if you are a pretty boy, you better be able to fight. I was good at it. I still am. I didn't take shit, from anyone. *Never acquired the taste for it, I guess.* If I thought you were going to do something dumb, I'd stop it, by any means necessary. But on the other hand, I was equally as charming, gracious, disarming and affable with a smile that would make angels heave a sigh. Just don't mess with me and we would be just fine. While I'm thinking about it, usually after school, my friends went to my home or I, went to theirs, to watch TV. One friend, Walter B., and I were watching something like the "Rifleman" starring Chuck Connors and we decided to make BLTs. While making the sandwiches, we sliced tomatoes, and toasted the bread. Well it was only a half tomato and we each took a slice and there was a half slice left, I reached for it with my hand and Walter reached for it with the sharp knife to pick it up and accidentally sliced my little finger on my left hand. I never told my parents or got it looked at. In those days, shit happened, and we just kept it moving.

Anyway, skip to today when people see my live show or me on YouTube, or anywhere, my left finger on my left hand is always sticking out as though I'm in England having high tea. It's because it never healed, and this is the result. I have been told it's an affliction, or I'm showing off. Wrong People always gave me what I wanted, and I'm blessed to say they still do.(I'm so grateful to possess that quality.) I remember when I was in school in the 60s, the boys were in charm school, we had to learn 'proper etiquette', we were in social groups like **Jack and Jill**, there were copies of Emily Post and Amy Vanderbilt on our coffee table which was read. In fact, if memory serves me correctly the wonderful actress Lynn Whitfield and I were in the same Jack and Jill group.

Back to my fighting. and trust me I'm not proud of it, but it's a part of my life and should be discussed. Writing this is kind of a catharsis for me. It had gotten to the point where I just lost all interest in school. The teacher would call on me to answer a question and I'd be looking into space, out of the window into La-La land. She would say Kanard, Kanard, (remember that's what I was called as a child growing up) finally someone would nudge me and say, she's talking to you. I'd get haughty and say what is it now? My hand is not up, why are you calling on me again? The teacher would say to me 'what are you thinking about, why aren't you listening', did you hear the question? Where is your mind? She was clueless to the fact that I was only in there because I had no choice. I wanted to say what Rhett Butler said to Scarlet, 'Frankly my dear, I don't give a damn'.in the classic film "Gone with The Wind", 1939.

So, I would say to the amusement of the class I'm thinking about what I'm going to do when I get to Paris. What I'll do when I get to Japan, London or Rome, or Egypt. Wherever my mind would take me. The class would all fall out laughing and say,

'Kanard so stupid', he's so crazy'. And I'd look at them like they all had two heads. And get back to the business of planning my world on my terms whether they or anyone else got it or not. By the way, my family also thought I was a bit out there, but secretly I believe they understood and got it. They just didn't know how to deal with it.

My way of thinking was just so unconventional. Still is, I'm happy to say. I'd goes nuts trying to conform. As Sammy Davis sang, "I gotta be Me:" in 1968. A big hit for him.

In high school, I started dabbling in drugs. smoking grass, which elevated into drinking cheap wines, 'Swiss Up', Bali High', 'Thunderbird' and 'Tokay', you could get a gallon for 69 cents on Swan St. And I was also smoking cigarettes in those days which were 33 cents a pack. God this makes me sound so old, like the stories my father used to tell me.

One day I went to a party in the neighborhood and got drunk off beer and wine. I was so drunk I had to crawl home, and the entire planet was spinning in my head. Stupid teenage stuff. I think I may have been 15.

I promised God and anybody else who would listen that if you just make the room stop spinning I wouldn't drink beer and wine again. Well in time the room stopped spinning, and I didn't drink for several years until I found myself on the left bank of Paris, and very expensive champagne flowed like, well, very expensive champagne. More about that later. (However, I never drank wine or beer again.)

I was 15 in April of 1968 when Dr. Martin L. King was assassinated that spring. Bobby Kennedy was assassinated 2 months later in June of that same year, five years after the assassination of Civil Rights Activist Medgar Evers in June of 1963, four years before the torture and murder of the three Civil Rights Workers - James Chaney, Andrew Goodman, and Michael Schwerner -killed by the KKK for registering Blacks to vote in Neshoba, Mississippi in 1964. Because of their deaths, and so many before them, President Lyndon Johnson and the Civil Rights groups were able to push through the Passage of

The Civil Rights Act of 1964 and the Voting Rights Act of 1965. This is why it's so important for the youth to vote today. Sankofa.

I'm so proud that I marched for Civil Rights in the mid - late 60s, it helps shape the person I am today. We had major demonstrations at Southern University, and I was right out front. The Vice President of the university, Leon Netterville, made me get in his car and drove me home. I went right back.

Back in school, I didn't study in class, when it was time for the test, and I had to pass to move on to the next grade. Because I was a pretty boy I'd flirt with the girls and they would always let me copy their answers off their paper. Like Maurice Chevalier sang in the wonderful 1958 Movie Gigi "Thank Heaven for Little Girls," for little girls get bigger every day. Most times it worked, other times it didn't. On rare occasions.

I was so damn tired of going to summer school, I really had a strong dislike for it. And because I kept flunking out, I had to go most summers. Not my finest hour.

I think I went to summer school two- three times. It messed up my summers. During this period my parents had big parties in our home often, like every weekend. Because my father was in banking, there was lots of entertaining going on; and our home was a popular place, for all of us kids' friends. Our friends loved to hang out at our home to gamble. Makes me laugh today when I write this, booze, weed, Jazz, Blues, fancy cars, pretty men and women, gambling, a real home. But not Norman Rockwell's home.

Often, my older brother's friends would come over, we would play Poker, Blackjack, Tonk, and sometimes if I lost my money, I'd run them out of the house with a hammer. What fun we had. I can still see Chucky running down the street laughing, and me chasing him.

It wasn't so much losing my money, but they would tease me about losing my money, And I'd go off every time. There are some things you just don't do, win a man's money and then laugh at him? Hell no. I'd grab whatever I could pick up and chase them out of the house. Because all of my brother's friends were my friends, I was a kid and they were much older.

Jaron at 17

My mother was one of the best cooks on earth. Seafood Gumbo, catfish, Creole shrimp, smothered pork chops or chicken. And she was glamourous on top of that. In our home-like Fats Waller might say, 'The Joint Is Jumping', which he wrote and recorded in 1937. Words by the great lyricist, Andy Razaf. He also collaborated with Fats on 'Honeysuckle Rose' and 'Ain't Misbehavin'.

'Now, all through the week it was quiet as a mouse; but on Saturday night, they'd go from house to house", as Louis Jordan sang in the classic 'Saturday Night Fish Fry' in 1949'. I recorded it in 1994 on my first CD, "Suddenly". Legendary Rock N Roll giant Chuck Berry said: "Louis Jordan was the first person he heard play Rock N Roll". But to me, truth be told, no matter what one called it, it Swung, it jumped, whether R&B, Blues, Old School, Rock N Roll. It was all soul music."

It was during this period when I heard and really listened to music in my home. My parents' collection. You see during the week, I heard my music, but on Saturdays, we had family house cleaning, each kid had a chore. And my mother who had a wonderful singing voice and could whistle in perfect harmony would put on her music. And that's when I heard real Jazz/ Blues.

It was 1965, I guess, and I heard a singer named Nancy Wilson sing "How Glad I Am". My entire world changed. To this day I have no idea why it had that kind of effect on me.

And then I heard a band called Count Basie, and Sonny Stitt and Grant Green, Ray Charles, Oscar Peterson, Lou Rawls, Dinah Washington, Nat Cole, and Sarah Vaughn and Ella. Pops and I were hooked, completely and unequivocally hooked. That sound grabbed me and hasn't let go yet. The sophistication, the elegance, the different depth I heard from this sound was positively majestic. At one of my parents' parties, Lionel Hampton who was performing in town came by our house and we were the 'Talk of The Town' (as Dakota Staton would turn into a hit in 1961, with Norman Simmons on piano.

In my sophomore year, I got into another fight over who knows what, and the principal said enough and expelled me from school. My father being who he was could have gotten me back in, but all concerned thought it best that I attend this semi-private boarding school in Lafayette, Louisiana called Holy Rosary.

It was a very good school, run by Catholic priests and nuns. Big stately building sitting on lots of grounds. The boys were in one wing, the girls in the other. I slept in this big barn-like building with many other boys. It was a boarding school where middle-class kids went who had attitude problems. I guess I fit the description. In fact, the great Rock and Roll -Soul singer Fats Dominoe's kids were my roommates - Andre and Antwine. I don't mean to dwell on fighting, I'm really a peaceful loving, kind man; however, if we are being honest, I need to tell what has happened in my life, which led me to where I find myself today.

My parents brought me to my new school. We met the headmaster or whatever he was called. His name was Father Oliver. And he looked at my records and said in a thick German accent, "Ja-Ron (my name on my birth certificate was spelled Jaron Kanard Eames), pronounced Jaron' but he insisted it was JaRon, so he named me JaRon. l liked it and it really was who I became or who I always was. I had never been away from home in this kind of setting and I was not amused.

The other students looked decent enough. Many from New Orleans, some from Chicago, Texas, Midwest. How they heard of this school was news to me. I had two friends who went there the year before me, Robert Anderson who was a dentist in Baton Rouge, and whom I hadn't seen since then, and Dart Thurman. Both have passed. It's 2019 now and I just did a tribute to Bobby Short, (the café society singer at the legendary Café Carlyle for 35 years) produced by playwright Calvin Ramsey, and I tell the story about how I auditioned for a play in high school (Moon River) and how they chose Robert to sing the song, "Moon River" and not me, and how I never recovered. It still gives me nightmares. I can't tell you how much I wanted that part in that play. Maybe It was then that I decided to go solo?

I never auditioned for a part again, until 50 years later. Now that's madness. I admit it.

A wonderful Jazz singer, Vinnie Knight had a play called "White Diamonds and Black Pearls" which I was a part of for a few performances in 2017, *I think*.

There was a very pretty girl who I met and dated while at Holy Rosary I have remembered her name all these years and just now it left me. Let's hope I get it before I finished this book. Anyway, we hit it off and it was a fun time. Oh, I got it, it was Rudi, she was a year behind me, and we used to walk around the ground holding hands. She smelled lovely in the Louisiana sun, under the weeping willow trees, which were a real turn-on. She was a pretty Creole girl from Lafayette Louisiana.

I got sidetracked, let me get back to fighting. (Just for the record, I have never started a fight in my life) ever. I would then, and now, go out of my way to avoid any confrontation. One day, actually my first week there, all the guys were gathered in this recreation room. Many of them had been in school there for years. They were friends hanging out together, and in walks me. The new kid, the pretty boy. So being the gregarious boy I am, I stood near the pool table watching them shoot pool with the rest of the guys. Some said hi, others didn't. The room was full of male students.

So, one of the guys playing pool was named Lundy. He was the **'Leader of the pack'**. Another hit song from 1964 by the Shangri-Las. So many references are musical in my head and it always leads to a song, sorry, I can't help it. And it's the same thing with old Hollywood movies.

Sidebar-

> (I would like to host a TV game show with this theme. Like name that tune; but instead, two people have a conversation and see who can come up with songs from the words in the conversation, *just a thought.)*

Anyway

Lundy was a popular 'wanna be thug'(this was 1969), from some rough neighborhood in New Orleans. He was losing his pool game and not in a very good mood, I assume. He was about to take a shot and ask me to move. So, I moved. Then he came near where I was standing and nudged me with the pool stick and said, 'I asked you to move'. So, I'm thinking, maybe I'm just taking up a little too much space, (I was no more than 120 pounds, if that.)

So, I said Oh I'm sorry, with a big smile, which I have always had and still do, to this day. It's part of who I am, a happy person. I was born happy, I'm happy to say. So, I moved again, this time all the way on the other side of the pool table across the room, damn near in a different state. Wouldn't you know it, here comes this fool again poking me with that damn stick;. threatening me, and saying, I'm 'gonna kick yo ass'. Well, yours truly had just about enough of Mr. Lundy. I grabbed that boy and we fought, and we fought, and we fought some more. The kids screamed fight. We punched, and kicked, and choked each other silly. I beat that boy so bad they had to pull me off of him. And he beat me back. Now, remember, Lundy had been at this school a few years and had a reputation to uphold. I was the new kid on the block, and he wanted to show me and the other 'newbies' that he and his crew were in charge. Well, I felt I was born with a reputation to match his or anybody else's for that matter, and after I beat his ass he soon became a believer. (Now today, I would never do that. And I don't encourage anybody to behave like I did back then).

In those days, boys had normal fistfights. Today, everybody carries Uzis and machetes, and razors and guns) *The world we live in.* God Help us. Now today if this same scenario were to happen, the first time he asks me to move, I would've left the room. Period. In fact, I wouldn't have even been in there. I don't like crowds. After our fight, Lundy and I slowly became friends, and my status rose very high in school. When people realize that you can't be pushed around, they stop pushing. That's why I never understood the bully concept. Come at me one time incorrectly and I'll do any- and everything to stop it.

I didn't like this boarding school either. It was worse. As I've said, and reiterated school was not for me. I ran away a few times, back to Baton Rouge and my parents brought me back. I never told them that, later in the school year I was once sexually molested by one of the top priests at the school. He was a very important and connected priest in that town, and in this school.

My father would've made a major issue out of this, I'm sure. And mother would've done worst to him. It was a small town, so why make a big scandal. He was a priest, and it was all very weird and brief., and comical. Life goes on. By the way, this is the first time I have ever told this story in or out of print. It was just so unimportant. Unlike Jacqueline Susann's book and movie, starting Kirk Douglas, one of my favorite actors 'Once is Not Enough' 1975), I had enough, and I left the boarding school after that school year at 16. I went back to my old school, Southern University Lab School, where all of my neighborhood friends were, for my senior year.

"When I was 17 It Was Very Good Year," as I heard Lou Rawls sing in the late 60s. The song was written by Ervin Drake in 1961. It was originally recorded by the Kingston Trio, but Sinatra won a Grammy for best male vocalist in 1966 for this song.

I was going into my senior year at 17. My parents bought my sister a brand-new Mustang convertible. It was a magnificent automobile - 1968 blue with a white convertible top, which we called 'drop-top'. I was considered a rich kid, when I was growing up; but most of my friends were from the so-called 'wrong side of the tracks' - all Thugs, Gangstas, dope dealers. Once my mother asked me, "Don't you know any 'decent' friends?" I thought they were quite decent. I didn't hang out with many kids in my class, except Burtell.

I was friends with all of them, though; but I was in the fast lane, then and now. It's just my DNA.

Shortly after my sister got the car, (she was 20) one of the major Airlines called her and she became one of the first Blacks to fly with Eastern Airlines as a flight attendant. She was drop-dead gorgeous and a lady. Then and now. Could've been a high fashion model. She left for New York and the car went to yours truly. I was beyond happy. 17 years old, and the summer before my last year of high school, thank God.

One of my best friends, then and now, was and is Bert Davis. He was big-boned, as they say, smart, street, and book Wise; and as funny as anybody you will ever know. He is still one of my best friends to this day, still big-boned, smart, and funny as ever. But now, he is the pastor of his own church. So, I can't tell you all 'good' things we did back then. However, I can tell about me. I ended up in show business like I always knew I would, and he ended up a pastor, as he knew he would.

Pastor Davis is one of the movers and shakers in Baton Rouge, raised four wonderful children who are now grown family men and women and he has a lovely wife, Lynn.

Scandals in show business are common as mud. The old adage, (don't care what you print about me, just spell my name right). Anyway, I'll never forget one of the first things I did when I got the car was going to a party at a girl's house that I had a crush on. At this point in the book, I better start using 'alias' because all of these people are still around and mostly in the same small town with families and lives, so there's no need to open up their past with my madness. Many of the names in this part of the book have been changed to protect the guilty.

The girl I had a crush on was Joyce B. So, I picked up Burtell and we drove in my new drop-top, with music blaring, to the house of Stephany H. where the party was, and Joyce was there. Today when the youth drive by blaring music, it drives me crazy. So now, I can understand older people getting upset at me when I did it as a teenager. Live and learn. There were about 14 people, all couples. I don't remember who Burtell was with. The lights were down real low, and I think it was either blue or red bulbs. Some of us smoked joints, drank wine, and played 45s. One record, in particular, I'll never forget. We played Stevie Wonder's "With a Child's Heart", over and over and over, then played Stevie's "Purple Raindrops". We petted and felt each other all over; we kissed grinding pelvis to pelvis while she sat on my lap, tongue down my throat, swapping spit, sucking lips. By the time it was all said and done, I was a wet mess above the neck and below the waist, and so was she. Thank you, Stevie. "

> *'Man is the only animal that blushes or needs to'*
> **-Mark Twain**

There was another girl in my neighborhood, and we used to play house, but I won't elaborate, so I'll just think of Campbell's soup (Um Um Good).

By that time, I was getting heavy into Rock and Roll. Three Dog Night, Led Zeppelin, Grand Funk, Hendrix. Grateful Dead. Crosby, Stills, Nash and Young, The Who. And more and more drugs. I started selling grass, and lots of it. I started selling pills, and lots of them, uppers and downers. I used to take 'big-boned' girls to the doctor's. office and get a prescription for (weight /diet pills) speed tablets as we called them. I used to have friends who forged Rx (Doc White, comes to mind. He wasn't a doctor, but he could forge Rx with the best of em). I had Red Devils, Yellow Jackets, Quaalude, Amphetamines, Barbiturates, Seconal, Tuinal, Valium. I was like a portable drug store. Also, I was taking them by the hand full. On the streets, we called the speed pills' Raps', because it kept you up all night and you would be speeding and talking a mile a minute. I was taking 2-3 speed pills in the mornings to get to school, and 2-3 Seconal at night to come down, along with smoking grass all through the day. I was high almost every day, eight days a week, 25 hours a day. On some kind of drug. It lasted for years. Years later, I understood Neely O'Hara in the **Jacqueline Susann film of 1967**

'Valley of the Dolls', staring the great Patty Duke and the great and legendary actress Susan Hayward.

I was 17 and a senior in high school (I looked 14), but most of my friends were in their mid to late '20s and 30s and some of them in their 40's. Go figure. I had access to all the drugs in town. I was the banker's son and selling drugs from the trunk of my convertible mustang. It had gotten so hot, a Black cop told my father that I had to be cool. One time my parents found several pounds of grass in my room, and they wanted to flush it down the toilet, but being wise parents, they had second thoughts and said it may belong to someone else and they would be after me if it disappeared. How cool is that for parents. One funny story now, then in the deep south 1960s, it wasn't so funny.

I and a good friend Jimmy S. were driving through town in Baton Rouge after making a drug pickup.(I just talked to Jimmy this week, 50 years later, and he's with his brothers on a yacht.) His younger brother Maurice is a big businessman and enjoying life. The stories I tell are from 50 years ago.

Now, I was always a fast driver. I still am. But this day I was driving leisurely. So, we're driving on this two-lane road and this old White man behind me started blowing his horn. He was in this plain white car waving me over so he could pass, now this was 1970 in the deep south. But me being, well… me, said f--- you, 'I'm driving the speed limit', go around me, and gave him the finger. I thought he was just being an asshole, and like an asshole, I reacted. Well, this old White man reached under his dashboard and put a red flashing light on his car and the White southern police officer pulled us over. Now mind you we had just picked up several pounds of grass, which in those days we called dope. And what seemed like a shoe box full of pills.

Jimmy and I were scared shit less. As we say down south, "We didn't know whether to 'shit or go blind' (My mother used to say, well, close one eye and fart). Anyway, this fat White southern cop gets out the car and walks over to us with his hand on his gun and looks in the car on my side of the window and said, "I'm gonna tell you N.....rs something. Y'all real lucky today, cause I'm late for a very important appointment; otherwise I'd put you both under the jail and throw away the key." We bowed our heads very respectful and said, 'yes sum'. Had he opened the trunk of my car it was surely the 'hoosegow' for us. So, we got into 'character' really quick.

But let it be said for the record, were it not for drugs in my trunk, he would've had to deal with me in court. But I couldn't react any other way sitting on all the drugs I had in my car. We proceeded to drop off the several pounds of grass, get paid and have a good laugh at what had just happened. Baton Rouge is a small sleepy college town. We have LSU, Louisiana State University (the White University) and Southern University (the Black University). Lots of college sports, and partying, drugs and alcohol. It's just the culture. If you have ever been to New Orleans, you know it's all about the party. College towns are about drugs, sex, alcohol, food, and a party. Period. For most, learning was secondary.

The most popular Black club for the kids at Southern University was a place called Morecos. I loved that place, and to this day it's still my favorite place (like most of the other Black clubs of my youth it has long since disappeared). This nightclub was operated by a man named Mosses McDonald. (His daughter Mada was in my class and has done publicity for me when I'm in Baton Rouge in the past.) We still talk often. Mr. McDonald drove a big Cadillac, wore green, blue, red, leisure suits and a big diamond Pinky, with a Stetson hat. I loved him. Kind of like a Bugsy Siegel look, I would guess. I was too young to be in his club, but I'd sneak in.

He would allow me to have one fruit punch and then say, "Eames, it's time to leave now." I'd go out the front door and sneak in the back. He was my idea of a nightclub owner. Mac, as he was called, had the best jukebox in town, handpicked by him. It was replete with Nancy Wilson, (his favorite singer,) Sarah Vaughn, Ray Charles, Dinah Washington, Sam and Dave, Big Joe Turner, Muddy Waters, Aretha Franklin, etc. What a club. In those days, after the college football games, that was the place to see and be seen.

It had the best BBQ in town. Everybody was 'fly' guys and dolls. All the guys spent as much if not more time getting dressed than the womenfolk. Petting and Picking our big Afro's into place, and getting the right Polly Ester bell bottoms, and paisley print puff sleeve shirt, and' Iceberg Slim' hat cocked ever so slightly to the side. And let's not forget the platform shoes. Well, after all, it was a fashion statement, and someone had to make it. I'd make lots of money after the games selling drugs. I'd pull up in my 'drop-top' Mustang and I'd sell out in an hour. Then get my party on. I became addicted at an early age and like most addicts, I didn't realize it. It seemed that I needed speed to get up and get to school more and more and Seconal at night to crash/come down and sleep. I have always had an addictive personality. I still do. When I like something, I simply overdo it.

I remember once it was a slow period for drugs in town, and again during this time I had discovered, hard acid rock. Alice Cooper, Iron Butterfly and I loved it.

This particular night there was no drugs in town but Acid/LSD. Now I wasn't into that, but it was a dry spell and I needed something, so a friend, (well actually didn't know him) gave me a little piece of square paper and said just put it on your tongue and fly. I was used to doing lots of pills and grass etc., and so I said to myself, "self" how can something this small do anything to me. So, like a fool, I put it on my tongue, hopped in my car, and turned up Grand Funk and I was off to the races. Well, I'll have you know that after a while, here I am driving; and out of nowhere this heavy green slim started oozing up towards me from the hood of my car coming over the windshield. I felt like I was in a bad Japanese B picture.

At least that's what it looked like to me at the time, and it scared me to death. I pulled the car over at the club, got out and ran inside saying to anyone who would listen that some green monster was covering my car. Well everybody in town knew the youngest Eames kid, and all of my friends knew I had never done acid. I told one guy about this thing I had put on my tongue and he said, oh man you tripping on acid his voice turned into slow motion, and his face became distorted. Quite frightening.

He put me in his car and took me to another friend's house who was having a party; we called him sexy Barns, his name was Randolph and it seems everybody was saying, whispering actually, wow he's on acid, and again it sounded as though they were speaking in slow motion. They had weirdly shaped faces that were several feet wide with weirdly deformed features. And again, all I could hear was, he's on acid, he's on acid. They put me in a corner on the floor and I curled up and waited out the storm. It passed. I don't know when or how long, but thank God, it passed. I have never put acid anywhere near me again and I never will.

That was not a pleasant trip at all. Timothy Leary the controversial American psychologist in the 1960's and 70's encouraged the use of LSD for its therapeutic, and emotional benefits.

Personally, I find masturbation works best for therapeutic and emotional benefits. And it's natural. In fact, I think I'll call the

Governor and suggest a law should be passed for every American of age to take an hour a day to masturbate to calm down the country. Timothy Leary also coined the phrase "Turn on, tune in, drop out." President Richard Nixon, at that time described him as the most dangerous man in America. I don't know what the Timothy Leary set saw in Acid, however many did. But I'll never take it again as long as I'm Black. Very Scary!

Another memorable event that changed my life happened around 1971. I heard on the Black radio station WXOK that Nancy Wilson was coming to the Roosevelt Hotel in New Orleans. As much as I had gotten into Rock and Roll, my heart was still steeped in my love of Jazz/ Blues/ and Soul. That's who I am./ where I come from. My history. My future.

Which explains why I'm so passionate about it to this day. So here I am sitting in class, and the teacher is bothering me with the who, why, what, when, how, and other madness that I had no interest in. And people let me be really clear, school is very necessary. We live in a world today in which it's true more than ever. Also, it's the foundation of learning for most people. I just didn't happen to be one of them.

I beg of you, please don't read this book and think you can sit back in class and do nothing. That worked for me. But remember this is my story. I really can't think of too many things I got from school. Other than annoyed.

But again, students need school, I can't stress that enough. Please stick with it, it works. Don't do what I did, this is my life, my story, what I have done worked for me. You have to do what works for you. Over thirty-five years later when I interviewed for my Jazz TV show, in my opinion, the funniest man and the most insightful genius, and philosopher on the planet George Carlin. Our backgrounds regarding school and work were so similar, I said to him (I'd never let school interfere with my education). To quote Mark Twain. Mr. Carlin expressed to me that he liked that. I was happy.

I wanted the class to be over so I could get to New Orleans which was and is about an hour or so drive for most, but I get there in 45 minutes. I'd had about all I could stand of class for the day, and I wanted to get to the city (as it was called by people who didn't live in New Orleans). I parked the car and hung out in the French quarter before the show. I cut my last class and "Hit the Road, Jack". **A wonderful song written by Percy Mayfield in 1960, but it became a #1 hit for Ray Charles in 1961. He also wrote the beautiful blues ballad, "Please Send Me Someone to Love".**

I walked around people-watching. Speeding like crazy from the amphetamines. I kept speed or Barbiturates on me at all times, it's so easy to become addicted and think we can handle it, but in the blink of an eye, it is handling us. The French Quarter is full of hookers trying their best to get you to spend your money on favors, God bless em. I used to love to flirt with them, and once or twice I did spend a few dollars for the' kindness of strangers'. (As Blanche Dubois, played brilliantly by Vivien Leigh said in the classic film a 'Streetcar named Desire', a Tennessee Williams masterpiece in 1951. I made my way to the Roosevelt Hotel. I was always a swell dresser when going out to any club. In those days, all Black men dressed to the 'nines' as we say. My parents had movie-star looks, dress and personality, so I come by it naturally. But make no mistake about it, I was wearing Du-rags, cornrows, stocking caps over my Murray's to get the waves in the 60s also. The youth today think it's new.

Now I'm sure some folks are going, stocking cap over the Murray's to get the waves? What is that about.) Don't concern yourself with that, It's a Black thing. **Or as 'Deke O'Malley' played by the actor Calvin Lockhart would say in the wonderfully funny film from 1970** *Cotton Comes to Harlem* **(Is it Black enough for ya).** However, when it was showtime, we pulled out the fine threads. We knew when to 'dress up or down'. I believe many of today's youth would wear a DuRag or baseball cap with jeans to opening night at the Metropolitan Opera to see Giuseppe Verdi's La Traviata. Also, there was another popular style among black men during this period like in my brother Carl's case, he was Fried, Dyed, and Laid to the Side. Like many black men of that era, especially those in show business or the fast life. They were also called Conk, or Process.

I arrive at the Roosevelt Hotel and its lush. I mean lush, plush. Thirty-Five years later when I interviewed George Wein (founder of Newport Jazz) he said in his book, *My Self Among Others*, a must read, that the owner of the Roosevelt swore no N..... would ever stay in this hotel, this was in the early 60s when Mr. Wein was producing a festival in New Orleans. You can read about that in my first book *Historical Jazz Conversations*. Anyway, I make my way to the Blue Room in the Hotel where the show is being held.

I sat my seventeen-year-old self at a huge table under a massive chandelier, the band stuck up the opening and a voice said, Ladies and gentlemen, Ms. Nancy Wilson. I heard all of three notes when some big burly White man insisted that I had to leave and now. Not only was I underage, I was 17, and look about 14, I don't remember seeing too many folks who looked like me in that room (we are talking 1970 in the deep south). But again, I only was there a short while. I couldn't see very much, and it was cozy and dark. I was too young to be in the club. I have a habit of getting what I want, so I 'requested' ever so gracefully if I may stand behind the curtain to see the show. I managed to see/hear a few songs and another burly white man ran me out. But the seed was planted. And I knew this is the life

I wanted. Nancy Wilson was pure majestic (1937-2018). I have tried to live my life by the following Quote.

> *"The biggest celebrities are those who defined themselves, and then set to work elaborating upon their image"*

I left the Roosevelt in a state of unmitigated bliss. I could still see Nancy Wilson taking the stage in a white beaded gown looking like "The elegant star that she has always been". That voice, unmistakable, swinging, sultry, bright, breezy and full of bounce which stayed in my head until this day. I popped another pill and headed to one of my favorite Black-owned hang outs in New Orleans, called Masons, a Motel in downtown New Orleans which catered to a middle-class Black clientele. It was a classy joint. Great music, pretty women, and men, just a nice place.

Great New Orleans food, and atmosphere. The owner's daughter Dale later married the legendary attorney who slipped the noose from around OJ's neck, Johnnie Cochran. I met friends, one whom I hung out with often at Masons, Paula W. We partied and a few hours later I drove back home too pooped to pucker. I had school the next day. I'm glad I didn't take to Heroin. I tried it a few times, but it just made me down, way down.. I used to snort it. If you see people who shoot or snort Heroin, they can go into a 'lean', or a 'nod' which I found myself in one night across the street from a club sitting on a planter. I went into a lean after snorting a bag of Heroin and was 'bent' for several hours and never moved, yet never fell. The cigarette was still between my fingers. Amazing.

The 1960s

JaRon In New Orleans in 1971 - Photo- Joshua Lloyd 3rd

Shortly afterward a major rock festival came through town. It was billed as Woodstock 2. The official name was Celebration of Life It was attended by 50,000 people, and there was so much pot-smoking that folks in the next town got high when the wind blew in that direction. It was held in McCrea Louisiana, June 25, 1971. The biggest thing to hit the south in terms of a rock festival. Pink Floyd, John Lee Hooker, BB King, Joe MacDonald, Sly Stone, Taj Mahal, Chuck Berry, Browns Ville Station, Ike and Tina were all on the bill. I don't remember which ones showed up.

Well, I'll have you know that my father told me, "Son, I don't want you anywhere near that 'drug den'. Don't go." I said, "OK, daddy." (I can honestly say that was the first and only time I ever told my parents a lie.) I went in the family room and watched *Gun Smoke* or *Laugh-In* and prayed he and my mother would go to their room and watch TV, sleep or copulate soon, so I could meet my friends and sneak out to the festival. Three of the small-town hoodlums came tapping on my window. Jimmy S, Clarence B, and Mike B, who was called Dirty Girt. All from the neighborhood. As soon as the coast was clear, I tiptoed out of the house, and we pushed my car out of the driveway as not to start the motor. We got halfway down the block and hopped in and took off. It was about an hour's drive. We had enough drugs to supply the festival. It was a mess, we had to park about a mile away due to all of the people and cars. When we got there, it was rumored that a hole had been cut in a back fence so people could sneak in, which we did. Let the party begin, the bands struck up and the drugs lit up.

Civil Right demonstrations, drugs, Anti-War movement protest, Rock N Roll, the sexual revolution, it was just an exciting time to be alive. I loved every minute of it. We who were demonstrating for civil rights as teenagers in the 1960s and Blacks who lived in that era have a different mindset than people who came up in the 80s- 90s, with no first-hand history of what it was like, or they couldn't degrade each other in such vile ways as they do today and call it art. I don't understand this need today to tear each other down, it's a meanness in our society today and it's sad.

We left the festival in time to get home before my parents woke up. Now I was 17, but they were three years older than me, they were all 20 years old. So, they didn't have to be home the way did. When I got to my home, I turned the car engine off and glided into the carport next to my father's Sedan DeVille Cadillac and my mother's Eldorado Cadillac. I was 'pleased excused my language, 'f---- up'. I had done so many drugs I was half-blind from all we ingested. I tried to gain my composure and sneak back into the house and into my room. I put the key in the door ever so gently, turned it and the door opened. I sighed a sound of relief knowing my bed awaited me. It was June, and Louisiana is the hottest place on earth. (I have never liked air conditioning, I still don't, I prefer to sweat naturally, but that cold air felt so good.) I'll never forget how good it felt walking into the house that night. I closed the door, took a few steps in the dark trying to get my bearings and get to my sanctuary, and that's when my father turned on the light and there he stood in front of me.

I don't remember much else after that, the shock had set in and it was like I had stepped into the twilight zone, and Rod Sterling was singing a duet of "Tiptoe Through the Tulips" with Tiny Tim.

I know father said something to me, but between being caught and being high as a kite I mumbled very humbly, "I'm sorry daddy". He said, "Go to bed, son. We will talk about it tomorrow."

My parents were so f---n kewl. By the way, that talk never came. I'm sure they knew I would sneak out and go because it was a once in a lifetime event in our small town.

That was a great summer. We had a very big yard and we were one of the first to get a riding lawnmower. I do remember my father made me get up after only three or four hours of sleep and cut the grass. I assume that was my punishment. I took 2-speed pills to prepare myself for what was my chore every week. I hated it. All I had to do was sit and ride, but I hated it with a passion. It was pure torture to my 17-year-old thinking. I'll never forget when I left home for New York, I said to my parents that I will never cut grass again. And I haven't. When I go home to Baton Rouge my neighbor Deloris Robinson still reminds me of that statement.

I was dating a very pretty girl in the neighborhood. Up to that point, we had been petting and kissing and playing house and, and, and but not gone 'all the way'. I really liked her. Later that day my girlfriend (I'll name her for this book) Susy called and said to come over, she had the house to herself. It was finally time, what we had both been waiting for. I get there and we kiss. She said there wasn't much time, so we decided to get busy. I was still coming down from the festival, and still full of speed, no matter how hard I tried, nothing would happen. The speed had taken hold of my body and rendered me helpless in this situation. She was a beautiful girl, and now she's a beautiful woman. I felt I had let us both down. That incident had a profound physiological effect on me for a while. I didn't understand it. It's not something people talked about back then. When I asked an older guy about it and he simply asked, was I taking speed? I said yes. He said that it was the 'speed amphetamines' and that is one of the side effects of speed sometimes.

I finished high school in 1971. I was 18. I graduated last in my class. I'm sure they only passed me to get me out of school. I don't think I went to class much at all my senior year and I'm not sure what happens in schools today, but we had student teachers then, which I think their duty was to substitute or learn what teaching was about.

But if you remember back a few pages I said that most of my friends were older than me, (maybe that was due to the fact that I was the youngest of six kids and all of my brothers' and my sisters' friends were also my friends) and a few turned out to be my student teachers. We would get high and party all night in nightclubs and see each other the next morning in class. It was a riot. My favorite student teacher was Brenda Jones from Bradley Road.

I remember very little about my High School prom except that we had a party at a Hotel, but I remember little else. The girl I took was named Hermine Milligan, a nice young lady. I have not seen or heard anything from her since 1971. And so, help me God, she called me last week and it's August 2019. She and her husband are coming to NYC to see the Temptations on Broadway and wanted to stay in my home. Amazing. My old friend Burtell gave her my number.

In my senior year, I wrote in my senior yearbook,(which is on my bookshelf next to me as I write this) the best thing that ever happened to me up to that point was to walk down that long aisle to get my diploma. God, I felt free. You have no idea. All through school I felt I was in quicksand. I would look at most of my classmates and they all just loved school. I've always marched to my own drummer.

Quote

'It is unrealistic to expect people to see you as you see yourself.'

JaRon High school graduation 1971

I started making plans to get to New York. When it came to getting out of this small town and getting to New York City I had tunnel vision. You can read my high school graduation yearbook from 1971 to see what everybody in town who knew me and that's practically everybody, wrote in my book, things like "I hope you get to New York and become a star, or I hope you travel the world as you dream of doing, I hope you get your own TV show and nightclub as you want, etc. etc.

Most thought I was daydreaming, a select few knew I was on a mission. I was doing God's will for me.

'The Law of Success', says

> *Along with positive thinking, you should use the power of continuous activity in order to be successful. Every outward manifestation is the result of the will, to create dynamic will power, determine to do some of the things in life that you thought you could not do, attempt the simple task at first. As your confidence strengthens, and your will becomes more dynamic, you can aim for the more difficult accomplishments. Be certain that you have made a good selection, then refuse to submit to failure. Devote Your entire willpower to mastering one thing at a time. Do not scatter your energies, nor leave something half done to begin a new venture.'*
>
> *- **Paramahansa Yogananda***

After the summer I registered and enrolled at Southern University. I was going to be a Freshmen. I liked the idea of it a lot. But like gas, it passed. It didn't last long. I didn't get a single book for class, nor attend one class. Yet, I was on campus every day partying. The life of the party. I'm not sure why I even bothered to enroll at Southern University. I guess it was what was expected of me, which makes no sense because I rarely, if ever, do anything that is expected of me. It takes talent to play one's self.

I had one thing on my mind, getting to New York. But I was truly having too much fun hanging out on campus. I got my first job at the University library in 1969 and was promptly fired soon thereafter. (As I might have mentioned earlier in referencing George Carlin, and our similarity). I have been fired from every job I have ever had since then. It's now in 2019. I was supposed to register for the draft when I turned 18. But the US Government was sending folks to Vietnam. Can you imagine? Me in Nam? I can't, and I have a very good imagination. Many of my friends who went to the army came back nuts.

Maybe that's too strong of a term. Let's say they came back changed and not for the better. Many were walking the streets talking to themselves, shell-shocked, it was sad. If they came back at all. I was doing a damn good job of driving myself nuts right here in Baton Rouge, thank you very much. And without going that far. One of my classmates and neighbors blew his brains out in his bedroom. Michael was a great guy, but when he returned, he was changed.

Besides, I took the Ali (Whom I dearly love and got to meet him in person when he visited my high school in the late 60's) approach "those people, the Viet Cong, never called me N.......they are not my enemy."

I also, like Muhammad Ali, considered myself a conscientious objector. Ali said, "Why should they ask me to put on a uniform and go ten thousand miles from home and drop bombs and bullets on brown people in Vietnam while the so-called Negro in this country are treated like dogs and denied simple human rights?" Say amen, somebody.

I don't have a fight with them. He was saying the enemy was right here in his own country. We needed to fight for civil/equal rights here in our own backyard. After my refusing to register, later that year they came to my home looking for me. In 1972 there were more and more conscientious objectors throughout the country. (The great actress Jane Fonda was a part of that movement, and all these years later, she and Lilly Tomlin have a hit show now on Netflix)) the government had its hands full. It was winding down and by 1973 the draft was ended. Thank God. I didn't have to move to Canada.

I was driving my blue convertible mustang on Plank Road in Baton Rouge, Louisiana and this old White man in an even older car ran into me and totaled my magnificent automobile. He reminded me of the scene in which Spencer Tracy and Katherine Hepburn were at the Ice Cream fountain in 1967 **film "Guess Who's Coming to Dinner"** (Starring Sydney Poitier) and he ran into a guy's car. My new Mustang convertible was no more. He was driving something from the civil war and not a dent in his steel Jalopy. It was the fall of 1972. It was also time for me to leave town for real. Maybe this accident was God's way of getting me out of town. Telling me it's time to go. Without my car, I was lost. If one lives in a small town without a car, God help you. And besides I made that promise to myself, when my parents brought my sister and me to New York in 1964 that when I turned 19, I was moving to New York. Well, I was 19.

My sister was working with a major Airline based in Newark New Jersey. In 1972 it was a nice place in the area she and her husband lived at the time, and from my understanding, it's getting much better with the new young Mayor Cory Booker, now Senator and Presidential candidate. She and her husband Alvin told our parents that when and if got there, I could stay with them until I got on my feet. That was all I needed. Alvin passed away in winter 2018. I liked him a lot, we had great talks, and arguments, and discussions for years. I was at their home every holiday since 1972.

If I said blue, he said red. His son Erik who is getting married to a lovely young lady in Vegas October 2019 is just like him. Alvin was a good friend and will be missed, I would have loved for him to have read this book so we can argue. He was a major help to me by letting me stay with him and my sister. By the way, Alvin and I used to go to summer school together in the late 60s. It was because of him that I recorded my first CD "Suddenly" in 1994. He told me to listen to this song, by the great soul singer Billy Paul called, "I'm Gonna Make It This Time". It was the story of my life and I got a band together and recorded it. Thank you, Alvin.

 I packed my bags and got one of my best friends we called Boo Boo (Joshua) Lloyd to drive me to the airport in New Orleans. (There is a photo on my wall in my red room of me in a big superfly hat, bell-bottoms and platform shoes, taken in New Orleans shortly before I moved to NYC, he took it.) We argued all the way to the airport, and the last time I saw him a few years ago, we were still arguing. This time it took a different turn and we stopped speaking, which is very sad. He got married and shit changed. We have a long history. Hopefully, we will be able to speak again. I stepped off the plane in December 1972 in New York City. It was showtime. I'd made it. I was home and I knew it.

Chapter 3

The 1970s

From the first time I uttered that statement "when I turn 19 I'm moving to New York" from my 11-year-old lips in 1964 after standing outside the **New York Hilton Hotel** and seeing the Beatles enter the Warwick Hotel across the street, I have worked diligently to make it happen. And everybody who knows me in Baton Rouge will attest to that.

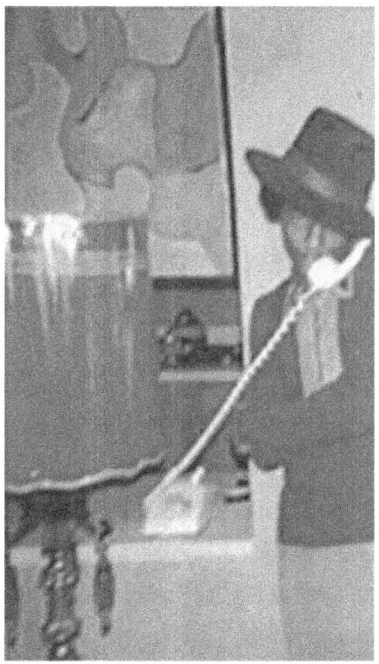

JaRon Arriving in NYC 1972

Alvin came to pick me up at the airport with a friend of his, Raymond. Alvin and Raymond remained friends all these years and he was at Alvin's funeral. When they met me, I was superfly for sure in my polyester bell-bottoms and fitted blue leather jacket, and player hat cocked to the side. After all, I was in New York City. At that time, they lived in a very nice apartment on the 23rd floor in Newark New Jersey. When I left Baton Rouge, I had a job as a salesperson at Sears and Roebuck; and of course, I got fired.

The last job I got fired from was the one at the college board located on Columbus Avenue and 62nd Street In NYC, a few weeks after I finished this manuscript in 2007, before the current rewrite. I was the overnight security guard 11pm-7 am. Each Job had its purpose for my being there. I used this one to start this book. I never was cut out for anything but show business. I accepted that years ago. In fact, I heard one of my favorite people, George Burns, from one of the funniest comedy teams in Radio/TV history, (1950 -1958) Burns and Allen say, "he would rather be a failure at something that he loved than a success at something that he hated." Watch Burns and Allen on YouTube, still funny after all these years.

Anyway

My brother in law Alvin was manager at a gas station, and he put me on at the station pumping gas (can you imagine)? I remember it was winter and it was cold and raining, I really did try my best to make this work. I was so grateful that my brother in law was in the position to get me to work that fast. But let's be honest, me pumping gas is like certain cable news station being fair and balanced. Ain't gonna happen. I think I lasted about a week, and that was too long. Here's what happened, A car pulls up to the gas station. It's bitter cold and raining and he says to me wash his windows. Well, I looked at him like he has 2 heads, and said it's raining. He wanted them washed and it didn't make sense to me; so, I said you wash them, and I went home. But I was 19 and at that age, we think we know all there is to know. And know so little. But I did know I wasn't going to wash his windows in the rain. I knew that much.

From their apartment, we had a clear view of Manhattan. I could taste it. I would sit in the window and say to my sister, "I can't wait to get there." She would say, it's too big and expensive and dangerous, so you should get a job over here and get an apartment here in New Jersey. I didn't tell her this, but I was thinking to myself, if I was going to live in New Jersey, I could have stayed in Mayberry with Aunt B. and Opie. Not that it's anything wrong with New Jersey; but for me, living anywhere outside of Manhattan would be like going to 'Fisherman's Wharf' and eating a fish sandwich from McDonalds.

I was so close to New York, just across the river. I would stare for hours, and hours at the lights and tall buildings. My sister, God bless her, would say things like "Apartments are much cheaper here in New Jersey, and the cost of living in NYC, etc." I would look at her like she had two heads, and say, "well, let's just see what happens", and I would get back to my dreams of what I plan on doing once I got to New York City. It became an obsession. Coming from a small town to the biggest city was a major move.

Once again, because my sister got a new car, she gave me her old car which was a Pinto. I would pop a few speed pills, smoke a few joints and drive into New York every day and look for work. At the end of the day, I'd take a few Valium Seconal or Quaalude to knock myself out. But being in New York, I was just too excited. All the years spent dreaming of getting here and now I'm driving through the Lincoln Tunnel heading into New York City.

I must tell you that driving through the Lincoln Tunnel drove me mad, completely mad, because I couldn't understand for the life of me how the Lincoln Tunnel was under all of that water, and every time I drove through it, I was a nervous wreck. All these years later, it still makes me nervous. We didn't have that in Baton Rouge, and for the life of me, I just couldn't understand it. I thrived on the energy of New York. The millions of people, the smells in the air, the noise, horns, traffic, it was like a circus. Like Mardi Gras 25 hours a day, 8 days a week. I was in heaven.

Quote
> *"Stay away from people who belittle your dreams, small people are good at that, Great people have a way of making you feel that you too can be great".*

I have always been blessed; and within no time at all, I had a job at a wonderful old record store, which is no longer in existence, called Sam Goody located on 43rd and 3rd Ave. It was one of the major chains, long before the mega stores of today. Working at Sam Goody's made me familiar with all of the Jazz and Blues artists, Classical, Rock, and Soul. I built a very good collection. I'm happy to say, I still have it.

One day a guy named Jon Schlissel came in to buy a record. I didn't know his name then, that came over time of his coming into the store. I sold him Johnny Hartman and Nancy Wilson albums. He came often after that and I would recommend albums for him and we became friends, he was one of the first friends I made in New York...my first New York friend.

And the first Jewish person that I knew of because where I was from in Baton Rouge, Louisiana we had Black and White folks, that's just the way it was. Now in New York, there are so many nationalities I can't keep up. Anyway, Jon and I remained very good friends. (When I make friends it's normally for a lifetime) In the first week of September 2001, we talked on the phone and made plans to meet in the coming week for lunch. But on 911 he was at work at the New York State Department of Taxation and Finance on the 87th. floor in the World Trade Towers when the plane came crashing through the building. I miss him terribly; he was a funny man with a good soul and great taste in music. *Thank you for being a friend.*

I'd worked at **Sam Goody's** for about 6 months, I guess (and was ready to leave or get fired, whichever came first.) when I met a kind soul while walking in New York. Like the tourist, I was looking up at all of the tall buildings, and millions of people. It was exactly what I'd fantasized, while sitting in class oblivious to the teacher, students, or surroundings of my youth in Baton Rouge. I was living my dream, my reality.

I met a group of very nice festive folks, well-dressed women and men, coming from a restaurant; and me being, well me, struck up a conversation, and asked which direction was so and so located. Pete answered and we talked about my being new in the city from Baton Rouge, etc., and would I join them all for a drink. At that time, I was drinking very little, if at all, since my beer drunk in high school many years earlier. So, I ordered juice. (I was full of pills-or as Jacqueline Susann wrote about, "dolls" my drug of choice).

When the evening was winding down Pete asked was I happy in the job I had. I said it wasn't a real job, meaning it wasn't a job that required much effort, not a career, I worked in a record store. However, I'm so grateful I did because it taught me so much about music and record labels, and sidemen on albums, which I use to this day in conversations on My Jazz TV show. God will give us the tools we need, even if we aren't aware of it at the time.

Tainted

He said there may be an opening at an Airlines and wondered if I would be interested in it. What does one say to something like that? I wanted to be clever and come up with a witty response and all I could muster, because I was still in shock, was "sure". I was 19, what did you expect me to say? Some Oscar Levant retort? One of his famous quotes among many was:

> "What the world needs is more geniuses with humility; there are so few of us left".

Well, a few weeks went by and I did hear from Pete again to come in and see the office and to get familiar with how things worked. I met the Director and Personal Manager, had some interviews, took a test, and after a few months I was an employee of Japan Air Lines.

NO BOOGIE — DBD staff in NYC's JAL Bldg. are busy with what looks like phonograph records but is actually a disk pack where information is stored. From the left is Jeff Choy, Pat Carner, Betty Tsutsui, Ja Ron Eames and Ron Farley.

JaRon working @ Japan Air Lines 1974

Once again, I was simply beside myself. In New York only a few months and here I am with an office on New York's premiere Avenue. The one and only Fifth Avenue, right across the street from Cartier Jewels which I could see directly out of my window.

"The Law of Success"

> *"Your success in life does not altogether depend on ability and training, it also depends on your determination to grasp opportunities that are presented to you. Opportunities in life come by creation, not by chance. You, yourself, either now or in the past (including the past former lives) have created all the opportunities that arise in your path. Since you have earned them, use them to the best advantage."*
>
> *- Paramahansa Yogananda*

It was late in 1972 and I was on my way. Movie star looks, personality to spare, charming and personable, making money and flying all over the world. As Adison Dewitt, played by the great actor George Sanders, who was married to two Gabor sisters, said to Eve Harrington played by Ann Baxter in the most nominated film in Hollywood history, *All About Eve*, "It is just as false not to blow your horn at all, as it is to blow it too loudly".

I was 19 years old. You couldn't tell me shit. I always knew what I wanted, even as a child, and I went after it. I was doing computer keypunch operations and I worked with some very nice people, Japanese and Caucasians. We all got along well. Most had never worked with Black people before, and I'm not sure what they expected; but because of my upbringing, I felt at home wherever I was. Always polite, disarming, affable. And as long as you don't annoy me, we will get along fine. The same rules apply today.

Tainted

JaRon in Las Vegas at Nancy Wilson & Bill Cosby show 1976

I was the first and only Black person in that department, and from my understanding, the first at Japan Air Lines on Fifth Avenue, other than a mailroom worker. From a very nice man named Cal, I also found out that the company needed some 'color'. I assume due to affirmative action, and I was chosen. (Or I chose them). Be that as it may. I was there and having the time of my adorable young life. My parents flew to New York right away to meet my manager/department head and to see where I would be working and what I would be doing. We also went apartment hunting. I must say, from a small child, I always knew I wanted to live on New York's Upper East Side. Being from Baton Rouge Louisiana, I had no idea what that meant, no idea where it came from, perhaps a movie?

Magazine? All I know is that's where I felt I belonged. I would read magazines as a child and in the back section it had ads about NYC. Addresses and so forth, but it was all foreign to me. It's truly amazing, to this day, I just don't know where that came from. Nor did I know what the Upper East Side was or where. We went apartment hunting. My mother, father, sister and her husband, and found a lovely place on East 85th St off 3rd Ave 10028. My parents paid the month deposit, and security, plus a few months in advance. We got furniture and I moved into my first and only home since I left Baton Rouge.

This was 1972

I'm still here today. By the way, someone wrote KKK in small letters on the wall next to my apartment door. There were no other writings on any of the walls in that 6-story building, and it stayed there for 25 years until my building was renovated and I was relocated / (bought out after years of battle) next door to another building and a larger apartment under the same owners. Interesting. I figured KKK letters didn't bother them, it didn't bother me. More about my apartment later. In fact, all about it. I must say very few people would have survived the ordeal I went through to keep my home. But you be the judge.

One of my most famous neighbors was Jacqueline Kennedy Onassis (1929- 1994) whom I met a few times, which I'll talk more about in detail later in the book.

She lived on my street. I was at 85th off of Third Ave, and Jackie Kennedy lived at 85th and 5th. 1040 Fifth Ave. Also, in the area were the Metropolitan Museum and the Guggenheim Museum . It's called The Museum Mile. A wonderful book about early New York's social 'Old Money' scene written by Kate Simon, is '*A Very Social History*.

Good stories about the fortunes and misfortunes of Rockefeller. Vanderbilt, Frick, Astor, Du Pont, Carnegie, Mellon, Whitneys and more. Many from the original four hundred. A phrase coined by the very Prominent Ward McAllister. He and Ms. William B. Astor decided who was in society and who was out. Ms. Astor's grand ballroom in the mansion held four hundred guests, which is how the social index '**Four Hundred** 'derived in the late 1890s.

The Mayor's official residence was a few blocks east on 87th St., Gracie Mansion. And so much more. I loved the neighborhood more than I do now. All of my dreams were coming true. I thought I had arrived. Hell, I had. Can you imagine? All that I had dreamt about as a kid in a small southern town, all of my life was now coming true. I did well at my job. On the job training, really. I picked it up fast and was liked by the others I worked with. But the pills and grass were a daily occurrence and it was hard to get to work at 8 am after being out all night, getting high and partying. So, they moved my time from 8am-4pm to 9am-5pm, which went OK for a minute, but didn't last. So, the next year they moved me to 10 am -6 pm. I was increasingly getting itchy about my music and started hanging out in jazz clubs singing anywhere there was an open mike. For years I could be found in some dive, singing with a bad sound system, and even the worst pianist and singing loud and wrong, having the time of my young life. After all, that's why I came to New York to become a "star".

In the mid and late 70s, there wasn't a club that I didn't sing in, most are gone now, but it was great dues paying and I wouldn't change it for the world. I became frustrated with having to sit behind a desk and type all day, so much paperwork. I was doing ticketing and other stuff, which I don't remember now. I wanted to be on stage, wanted to sing, wanted to do what I came to New York to do, but Japan Air Lines was paying my rent, and allowing me to fly to Vegas, or San Francisco or Hollywood, for dinner, if I so choose. However, I was slowly getting bored with the job. I wanted 'it all' today. There's a commercial on TV nowadays saying I want it all, I want it now. It makes me smile when I think of my early days in NYC.

But it doesn't work like that. I found out the hard way; which brings to mind a wonderful film starring the great actress Ida Lupino (1918-1985).

Old-school hard-boiled actress, in the movie *The Hard Way,* 1943. She was one of the first female filmmakers in Hollywood. It was a very good film, if one likes that kinda thing. I just happen to love a story, a beginning, a middle and an end.

I must admit, working on Fifth Avenue was truly a ball. Walking up and down the Grand Avenue to and from work, spotting celebrities, people watching, being watched. It was marvelous. During this time, I was hanging out at a club, long gone, called the **Playboy Club**. I had a gold key, which meant I was a member, and that's where I would be often. It was located on 59th St. off Fifth Ave. Between Fifth and Madison Avenue. One night, I was sitting at the bar, high as a kite, and in the walks one of my college friends from Southern University, Jeanette L., who is still living in New York and working in fashion. *We talked last night.* We would pop amyl nitrite and disco dance all night in the Playboy Club. I'd take a few speed pills early in the morning to make it through work, and a handful of Seconal, or Tunnel to crash at night, and some of the best weed money could buy. I was introduced to a Doctor where I would get Valium, which came in handy because shortly after this period I lost my connection for my beloved Barbiturate, Seconal. Jeanette had a job as a salesperson at the famed Bergdorf Goodman, and her Co-worker was a very young, very funny, very tall, extravagant guy named Alex.

The three of us would often meet for lunch, usually in the summer sitting in Central Park and dreaming. Alex wanted desperately to be in high fashion. He would go on and on and on about his dream of runway modeling and fashion, etc. .He made it. Today you may know him as Ms. J. from the Hit TV show America's Top Model. We have a long history and some very funny stories of his entrances into Studio 54 in 'drag'. I respect him for going after his dream and making it a reality. And Jeanette L. is a patternmaker and making original designs. What times we had, but you can read his very funny book *Follow the Model*. I'm happy to say we are dear friends today and talk on the phone from whatever location he's taping from, and text frequently. I try to keep real friends for life. One has to be a friend to have friends. One day I was walking up Fifth Ave and saw this elderly, heavily made-up White woman, and she caught my eye. She was looking in the window of Gucci. Me being, well, me, said, "hello, aren't you Garbo?" During that time, Greta Garbo (one of the biggest stars of the silver screen, 1905-1990) used to walk all over New York. Later I did see her on Madison Ave. There were many Garbo sightings, however, this little woman looked me right in my eye and said, "No! Garbo is very tall, with big feet". I said, "oh, I'm terribly sorry, Ms. Swanson." It was Norma Desmond herself. The Silent film movie star, Gloria Swanson, 1899- 1983. She made her debut in films in 1914. Charlie Chaplin. directed her in a film. She was also the mistress to Joe P. Kennedy, President John F. Kennedy's father. Her most memorable line from the movies- "I'm still big, It's the picture that got small," from one of the best films about old Hollywood ever made, **Sunset Boulevard,** 1950. (Directed by the brilliant Billy Wilder. Co-starring William Holden, Erich Von Stroheim, and Nancy Olson).

I felt bad because I pride myself on knowing 'old Hollywood' or as I call it Authentic Hollywood.

I guess I was just so excited, and the wrong name came out. Today I have a large collection of old Hollywood classics, which I watch often, as you might have noticed from many of my references. I'm blessed that I got to meet a few of the legendary Hollywood stars in person. Like the time I met Barbara Stanwyck, on the right arm of William Holden, and Anne Baxter on his left arm. What a night. It was a tribute to Ms. Stanwyck, presented by ' **The Film Society of Lincoln Center' in 1981**. I got to shake hands and hear Ms. Stanwyck say in the heaviest voice of any woman I have heard, "so glad you came tonight." She had the trademark white hair, also wearing a white mink. I really was thrilled. And Ms. Baxter, 'Eve Harrington herself', one of the greatest if not the greatest, role ever written.' *All Above Eve*, **1950,** for any movie, in my opinion, saying in her most breathlessness, "thank you for being here". She had a way of talking, as though she was just about out of breath. And of course, Bill Holden was a Movie Star, looked the part and played the part. Unfortunately, in 1981 he died alone in his home drunk, after falling and hitting his head on a table and bleeding to death. His role in the classic 1955 film, *Picnic* with Rosalind Russell and Kim Novack was priceless.

When a celebrity is in the newspapers daily we feel we know them, and that's how I felt about Jackie Kennedy. Like we were old friends. Can you imagine? During that time, she was on the cover of every magazine, every day since President Kennedy was assassinated November 22nd, 1963 and up until her death on May 19th, 1994. During that period, two women were on the cover of every magazine in America. The other was Liz Taylor.

Anyway, Jackie (if you don't mind I'll call her Jackie like we were friends) worked right near me during this time. I was on 52nd and Fifth at Japan Air Lines, and she worked at 53rd and Filth, at Doubleday books. There was and is a wonderful hamburger joint called Burger Heaven located on 53rd between Fifth and Madison Avenues. I used to eat there often during my time with the airlines, and so did Jackie Kennedy.

I always wanted to see her in there but kept missing her. She had either left already or came in after me. I had befriended a waitress who worked there, and she kept me informed. The restaurant had her picture in the window as a frequent guest there.

One day I walked in and low and behold, she's sitting at the counter eating a burger. I was praying that the person next to her would finish his lunch and get out of my way. I could see he was almost done, but it wasn't fast enough for me. So, when it was time for the host to seat me, I pretended I was busy doing something and motioned for the person behind me to go ahead of me. This person sitting next to Jackie decided after finishing his burger, to have a piece of a pie. I wanted to slap him.

The person next to him left and I sat there. I figured it's close enough to American Royalty. She had ordered already. So, I ordered and because I throw my food down, then as I do now, we finished eating at the same time. (I planned it that way) .When I was growing up, my mother used to say, while watching me eat, "relax, we are not going to take the plate from you, it's plenty more." Jackie Kennedy got in line to pay her bill and she was right behind me. I was a mess, I turned into pure jelly. In my best Clark Gable voice, I said, Ms. Onassis, I would consider it an honor if you would allow me to buy your lunch today. She smiled a big smile and said, thank you, that's kind of you but I couldn't do that.

Now she had millions and I had barely enough to pay for my own lunch. Maybe It's a blessing she did say no, now that I think about it. But I will never forget that day. I had come face to face with

American political royalty and had a close personal encounter. For someone from the small town of Baton Rouge, it was a big deal. I couldn't wait to tell everybody about my day. In fact, I ran and told it.

Another close encounter with Hollywood Royalty, Political Royalty, and 'sho Nuff' Royalty, I believe it was the early 80s. I was coming home from Central Park on my bike and I saw lots of folks all dolled up going to the Metropolitan Museum. So, me being well, me, asked what was going on. I was told it was a tribute to the legendary entertainer Josephine Baker. I was just too impressed. I had just bought a black glamour mink coat. In the 70s, during the Muhammad Ali fights, all the 'Black players', and 'swells' had a mink coat. Clyde Frazier, the NBA superstar for the Knicks, Joe Frazier, one of the greatest Boxing Heavyweights ever, legendary Fight promoter Don King, legendary New York Jets Quarterback Joe Namath Sammy Davis, Burt Reynolds, and Isaac Hayes, to name a few. So, yours truly had to have one. Again, as Lou Rawls said, in his blues "I have to have my front so I can keep on making my game". I may have this date incorrect, but I think it was winter.

Since I'm telling my story I shouldn't leave out how I got the mink coat. I paid for it, I think it was on sale for $2000.00, I had them ship it to my friend's home in NJ to avoid the sales tax. I called my friend and said to be on the lookout for a package I was expecting. I also told her when to expect it. I called that day and the package hadn't arrived. So, I called Macy's department store and said my coat had not been delivered. So, they said, "yes it was, that morning". So, I called my friend again and said are you sure, she said, she wasn't home that morning, but let me look on the porch. She notices the dog playing with a box in the yard, she went to investigate and sure enough it was a new black Glamour mink inside. I said, "did you sign for it?" She said, "no." I said, "then you never got it." (People, please don't think badly of me for this incorrect act.) I called Macy's in a state of shock, saying I needed my coat and if you can't get it to me tomorrow, cancel it. They had to cancel it and give me back my money.

Today I still feel bad I did that. It was 1976. I was 23 years old, full of pills and drugs. And I figured Macy's has millions, and I had so little. *Why*, I said to myself, *not?* When I look around today at the Wall Street scandals, the banking scandals, the mortgage lending scandals, Fanny and Freddy bailouts. My goodness. Or as Mae West said, "Honey. Goodness had nothing to do with it". What I did was so minuscule in comparison.(I'm not justifying) just saying. Mae West was a true original. In fact, she loved jazz so much, that in one of her movies in the 30s, she wanted Duke Ellington's band in the film, but due to racism/segregation, the Hollywood head said no. But Mae was a big star with lots of power, and she said either hire Ellington, or cancel the movie. It was Duke's first big Hollywood movie and Mae West (1893-1980) made it happen.

Then I thought to myself, my little insufficient act was just that. What would you have done? At that age. Don't we all think we know everything at that age? I saw a chance to "get over" on a major department chain store. And besides, it was more money I had for drugs and parties. I don't remember where I met him, but I had befriended a coke dealer who became my supplier. He had a European accent, and some of the best coke around. He was also the supplier for a famous performer, who shall remain nameless (with a hit TV show and movie), who lived below him in Turtle Bay Towers on NYC's East Side. So that money came in handy. Now back to this grand party for La Baker. I got dressed in a black suit and threw on my **'What becomes a legend most'** mink and walked from my apartment a few blocks to the Metropolitan Museum.

I was young, but older and wise for my age. Growing up, all of my friends were older, and it rubbed off. The good, the bad and the ugly. This affair was being hosted by Myrna Loy, the great Hollywood actress who was famous for the **1934 *Thin Man* movies**, with William Powell, also Jackie Kennedy, and Princess of Monaco Grace Kelly, who was so instrumental in helping Josephine Baker in her time of need.(she was a real friend to her in many ways). An addendum, Grace Kelly was simply radiant in one of my favorite films ***High Society*, 1956**, with Bing Crosby, Frank Sinatra, Celeste Holm, and the scene stealer, Louis Armstrong. When the movie opens, the band is on a bus and Pops is sitting on the back seat swinging the title song, "High Society". Words and music are by the brilliant Cole Porter.

It was Grace Kelly, her husband Prince Rainier of Monaco, and Jacqueline Kennedy who financed Josephine Baker's last performance at the **Bobino In Paris** for her 50th Anniversary in show business.

The show opened on April 8th. 1975. It was a major success. Ms. Baker was the talk of the town. Four days later, she was found in a coma, in bed with newspaper clippings and rave reviews scattered everywhere, about her concert. She had a cerebral hemorrhage and died after being taken to the hospital on April 12th, 1975 at the age of 68. How grand is that? What a way to make your exit, take your final bow, then by reading great reviews of one's self. *There's no business like show business*. Back to the party at the Met.

I, of course, was not invited to this big fancy party, but me being, well me, never let little things like that get in the way. I always take the long view. So, I entered this gala and heads turned to see who this young black kid in the mink was. Nobody asked me anything, like where is your invitation, (this was the good ole days before 911 and over the top security which we seem to suffer nowadays.) I started a conversation with someone who was from the press and when they did the seating, I was seated with the press. I did get to meet Myrna Loy, and she was very elegant, graceful; but I remembered she had freckles on her back./shoulders. Isn't that an odd thing to remember? Princess Grace Kelly was a vision of loveliness. Like "an alabaster palace, rising to a snowy height" (a great song lyric from the hit song **"Midnight Sun"**, written by Lionel Hampton and Sonny Burke in 1947 with Lyrics by the great Johnny Mercer). We shook hands and talked like we had known each other for years. She didn't have to spend time with me. A class act.

And my 'very good friend', Jackie Kennedy was drop-dead, yet understated glamorous. I reminded her of the time in Burger Heaven, she said she remembered., but I think she was just being polite. She was very pleasant. The event was to celebrate La Baker's wonderful life. I'm blessed to have been a part of this evening. I swear it became delusional with me, almost an obsession because I even found myself hanging out at this joint called **PJ Clark's** on 3rd Avenue and 55th Street, simply because Jackie Kennedy was there often in the late 1970s and early 80s.

Once I sat at a table next to her. I never bothered her or intruded on her space, but it was just wonderful being in her energy. I'd say what I had to say and move on, never demanding her attention or recognition. I'm sure many were pulling at her. Must be awful being so famous. But she was always a lady. I guess I was just playing out my fantasy, which was, in reality, my reality. Also, for a short while when I was working at Japan Air Lines she would visit next door at the Olympic Towers located on Fifth Avenue and 51st St. (Owned by her Greek Billionaire shipping magnate husband Aristotle Onassis 1906-1975).

So, it seemed she was always around, or rather I was always around where she was and again when you see these people in the news daily you think you know them. That they are your friends. Is that sick or what? Looking back on it, I'm surprised she didn't have me arrested for stalking her or take me to court as she did Ron Galella, the famous paparazzi-style photographer. The final outcome of the legal proceedings was that Galella was ordered to stay at least 50 yards away from Mrs. Onassis and 75 yards away from her children. But I must say on the occasions that I was blessed to meet her and exchanged words, she was always gracious. Ever so the lady. After her death on May 19, 1994, my mother happened to be visiting me and we stood outside of her apartment, which was a 5-minute walk from my apartment, with 100s of other people in what was a very emotional night for all present. And when John Jr. died in that plane crash in 1999, that was truly like losing a family member. We watched his father's assassination. The Kennedy's were a part of the American fabric.

America felt we knew them. I had an accident on my bike with John Jr. in Central Park. He was an avid bike rider also. For those of you who know Central Park, we were going down that hill north of the Metropolitan Museum off Fifth Ave. and we bumped our bikes. A really good guy.

Another time I happened to be biking in Central Park, (after all it is in my backyard), and I saw this older gentleman walking alone. I, of course, recognized who he was, so I got off of my bike, approached him and introduced myself extending my hand. I said Mr. Tempelsman, My name is JaRon Eames. Maurice Tempelsman is a wealthy, Belgian-born industrialist and diamond merchant. He also handled Ms. Kennedy's Finances, quadrupling the $26 Million she received from the Onassis estate. I was wearing biking shorts, sneakers, no shirt and a baseball cap turned backward, as so many New Yorkers do while biking. This gentleman was deep in thought, so I didn't want to take up much of his time, but I felt compelled to share my feelings with him about the wonderful job he did in helping to plan Ms. Kennedy's funeral. I wanted to simply thank him.

He was her companion and shared her Fifth Avenue home for many years, until her death. I bring this up because I wanted to say to him all of these years later, that I'm sorry if I was in error. Here is what happened. Before I left him in the park that lovely day, I said to him would it be OK if I send you a copy of my newest CD, "Suddenly". He thanked me for my kind words regarding his planning of the funeral and said he loved Jazz and he would look forward to receiving my CD.

I sent him a copy and I received a wonderful letter on his stationary saying that he enjoyed it. Well, we became pen pals and exchanged several letters/notes for two years. When I was assaulted by the NYPD in 1996, (I was pulled off my bike and slapped and handcuffed) I won a small settlement from the city. He sent me a lovely note expressing his concern and prayers. Then once, I believe it was around 2001, I was going through a mild depression due to my career; and in a letter to Mr. Tempelsman I was thinking out loud but putting it on paper. I asked him if he would be interested in investing in my Company JKE Productions. I think it was a mistake because after I asked him to invest, all letters stopped. My upbringing was very middle class. But this was wealth and I guess it was a cardinal sin to ask for an investment. I guess that world of wealth was out of my reach, and if I was in error please forgive my lack of protocol. I still have all of the wonderful letters we exchanged, and I cherish them. Speaking of wealth. Let me relay one more story before I get back to the business at hand. There's so much in my head.

I read in the society papers that a special birthday was coming up that August. So, me being me, I got on my bike and took a CD to Mrs. Brooke Astor of the Astors, **the American philanthropist and socialite.** She was turning 93 years young. She died at the age of 105 in 2007 in squalor, due to her son Marshall who also stole money and paintings, according to his son who started the case; and later Marshall went to prison, which I thought at his age was shameful. A sad scandal indeed. I ran into his wife Charlene on 3rd Ave. once and merely said how sorry I was that they all had to go through this public nightmare. (The same judge who sentenced her son to jail, Judge Kirke Bartley, also sentenced me to jail a few years later. But more about that in time.)

I did not put my CD in Mrs. Astor's hands personally, I left it with her doorman on Park Avenue. But a few days later I received a very sweet note on her stationary telling me that Ms. Astor was at the summer house, but she would get my CD to her, and thank you. It came from her social Secretary, Lorene Latine, on Ms. Astor's Blue stationery. We exchanged a few letters, and for that, I'm grateful and blessed. Looking back, I ask myself how did I know these people and develop a relationship with them. But the only thing that makes them different from you and me is money. Mrs. Astor lived to be 105 years old. How she was treated in her later years by family became a major scandal in New York at that time.

But I digress.

Now back to JAL. In mid-1977 Japan Air Lines moved my work hours from 12-8pm. I still couldn't make it to work because I was in the clubs all night living my dream, (Also, often I was full of coke, and pills). So, after four years, we both decided it's best if I made a choice. Japan Air Lines or my music career. I chose to follow my dream of show business. (I haven't been able to rub two dimes together since). I'm not one for looking back, but had I stayed in that job I would be retired today with a nice fat pension and free travel for life. But I'm sure I would have gone completely mad or would have gone postal, had I stayed. I need to be on stage, period. I need to create, period, I need to express, period. And I have always known it.

"No complaints and no regrets, I still believe in chasing dreams and placing bets. But I have learned that all you give is all you get, so you give it all you got. **"Here's to Life"** is such a beautiful song, written by the brilliant Artie Butler. Thank you for this jewel.

It was settled that I get an open ticket and I could travel around the world. My trip lasted a little more than three months. The ticket was part of my leaving package. I didn't have any money, but I had a few credit cards like Carte Blanch, Diners Club, and a few others. I put them all too good use. I had gone to Tokyo, Hong Kong, Hawaii, Alaska and most of the Caribbean Islands, the years before. I used to fly to Vegas, and Hollywood for 12 dollars just to have dinner and see a show. The last show I saw in Vegas was Nancy Wilson and Bill Cosby. I was living large, often full of coke and hooked on pills daily.

JaRon in Paris 1977

When I started what I call my world trip, I don't remember what order or direction I flew, but I went to London. I was there during the **(queen's 25-year anniversary 'Silver Jubilee'.)** That was where I met and had dinner/drinks with the great lady herself, Mable Mercer. Frank Sinatra used to listen to her and study her phrasing, or so it's been reported. She was performing at **the London Playboy Club,** and I was a gold key member here in the New York club, so it was good at any Playboy Club. I got to watch/study her show and she was majestic. Regal, in fact. She saw me at the bar, after her performance. I was the only person of color in the room, I believe, other than Ms. Mercer and a member of her band.

She sent one of the guests at her table to the bar where I was seated and asked me would I join her table. (Now that's class, folks). I did, in fact, join her party; and it was a night to remember. Me at Ms. Mercer's table in the London Playboy Club. I started singing to myself, Tadd Dameron's **"If You Could See Me Now"** because I'd heard Sarah Vaughn sing it earlier that week. In fact, he wrote it for Sarah in 1946.

I left there and went to a hip jazz club that's still swinging today, Ronnie Scott's. I don't remember the band that was there, but it was happening. I stayed in London for a week, then I flew to Rome, Venice, Bangkok, India, Egypt, Amsterdam, Copenhagen, Iran. In fact, I was in Iran in the summer of 1977. It was the prelude to the taking of the American hostages, which happened in 1979 until 1981. Islamist students took over the United States Embassy in support of the **Iranian Revolution**. The 66 hostages were held 444 days. I might have been hostage # 67. Here's why.

I was staying at the quaint Excelsior Hotel when I got a frantic knock at my door, I opened it and the hotel manager said to me excitedly "I must leave the hotel right away". I said, "why must you leave the

Hotel right away, and why are you telling me, a total stranger your plans?"

Leave the hotel right away, OK? He meant that I had to leave right away. Me. So, I'm still not getting the severity of this, and I'm still making light of the situation. Now I'm in my 'Hollywood mode', saying to him "why must I leave? Is there no more food in the pantry? Have they padlocked the doors? I must know." Something I thought Groucho Marx might say. (I watch the Marx Brothers' movies often, soooooo funny.)

There's a car waiting to take you to the airport now. By then I could tell from the sound of his voice and his demeanor that this was serious, and I better get my things and get going. Well , I threw things into a suitcase and I got in the back of this waiting car/taxi. And we started out to the airport. By this time, the streets looked to be filled with thousands of Iranians burning American flags, and effigies, screaming "death to America, and America, the great Satan…" and so forth. And here I am in the back of this car, trying to hide, scared to death, clueless as to what's going on, but knowing that I wanted no part of it. I mean I do love drama, but this was over the top.

It really did have traces of the Hollywood classic *Gone with The Wind* and I thought I was in the movie (an updated version). By the way, each character in the movie was brilliant. Hattie McDaniel's Profound performance as Mammy made her the first African American to win an academy award. And who could forget the lovely Butterfly McQueen as Prissy? Two marvelous Black actresses forced to play maid roles and other servants, still brought dignity to their characters. Ms. McQueen, an atheist, died a horrible death due to fire in 1995. Of course, Rhette and Scarlet brought magic to the performance.

When the film opened in Atlanta the 'good white genteel folks' in the city refused to allow Hatti McDonalds to appear with her co-stars due to strict racist segregation laws. Clark Gable said if Ms. McDaniels is not going to be with the cast then I'm not going, supposedly she encouraged him to attend. The Hollywood premiere was equally as disrespectful, but she was allowed to attend and sit at a table in the back of the room and not with her white costars up front. *But this is American history.*

The film was hated by many blacks, but it was a time in America and her performance was simply brilliant, done with profound dignity, and a good story. As Hatti said," I'd rather play a maid than be one'. It was 1939. I have to watch movies of that period and leave politics behind. It took Hollywood twenty-five years before it awarded another Oscar to a black person which was Sidney Poitier for best actor in 1964 *Lilies of the Field*, and another black women Whoopi Goldberg in 1990 for *Ghost* a full fifty years after Ms. McDaniels.

Forgive me, once again. I digress. Back to Iran.

All of a sudden, the car I'm in is stopped by the demonstrators. We are surrounded and the door swings open. I looked at the driver, he looks at me, we're both helpless, me more so than he. I heard a voice, "he's an American, take him." They pulled me out of the car, and we were standing eye to eye. Me and my captors.

Without missing a beat, I held up my arm and put it next to his arm and said I'm not your enemy, I'm just like you. Your fight is not with me. I'm a Black American, I'm discriminated against in my own country; your issue is with the American government. He looked me in my eyes and said, "let him go." I sat in the back in the car in a state of shock, that my comments possibly saved my life. Surely saved me from becoming a hostage. (I believe street smarts are more important than book smarts in these types of situations). Thank God for my upbringing, and quick thinking enabled me to talk/act my way out of many issues. I will never forget that experience.

We seem to have just enough religion to make us hate, but not enough to make us love one another.

My next flight: in no particular order, I flew to Amsterdam, Bombay, Copenhagen, Greece. I was all over the place. It was in Greece where I learned that Elvis had died. I saw it on the cover of a magazine while walking downtown to a newsstand. Another interesting story. While in Greece, I was nude sunbathing on a lovely white sand beach, one of my favorite past times.

I'm lying on my back, arms outstretched, in heaven, soaking up the sun. All of a sudden, I hear this very loud horn-sounding noise, I turn around and it was maybe 5000 people all waving and cheering me from a major luxury ocean cruise liner about 50 feet away. They were so close I could almost shake hands. I waved back and continued to enjoy nature. If that happens in America, they arrest you. Go figure.

Bangkok was my next stop. I had a lovely room at the Opulent Dusit Thani Hotel. One of the grand Hotels in Thailand. The second night there, I picked up a hooker, took her back to my Hotel. We got high and had sex, then I felt her trying to undo my gold chain from my neck, as we lay in bed. The slut was trying to rob me while I'm still awake, she couldn't even wait until I was asleep. I threw her out into the hallway. As an addendum, I just found a photograph I snapped of her putting on her panties, but I can't put it in this book.

One night while walking in the downtown area after dinner, an army truck passed by, gave me the once over, and stopped. Out jumped two army guys in full regalia and guns. I was waiting to see the action, some excitement, I couldn't understand why the streets were so quiet I was the only one out, a weird feeling. Anyway these army/policemen said something to me in their language, then put me on the back of this big truck taking me to what ended up being the hoosegow .I'm sitting in the back of this army truck in a 3-piece chocolate lightweight summer suit, eggshell/cream-colored shirt, pocket square, tan loafers, and cigarette holder, 'Think Humphrey Bogart'. Next to me were local street people and we looked at each other like we all had two heads.

Unbeknownst to me, it was martial law and curfew at 11 PM, which the Hotel apologized profusely for not telling me. I'm sitting at the police station, not speaking the language and we're just looking at each other. I must admit I did look like I 'just stepped out of a bandbox'. Finally, the Hotel manager came to get me. And all was well on the Bangkok front. Bangkok was a place where, in those days, many rich Americans went to get diamonds and other jewels. I had no money then, nor do I now, but that's never stopped me before. It's merely an inconvenience. I have always lived by this rule, 'A man who lives within his means, suffers from a lack of imagination'. I had major credit cards. And used them well.' (I don't recommend people do what I did, As Flip Wilson's/Geraldine used to say, **"The Devil Made Me Do It"**) The "Dolls" I was popping daily surely affected me. In fact, one reason I'm writing my book is, so others hopefully won't travel down the destructive path of Drugs and booze that almost killed me.

I bought what seems like a bag of Diamonds, for family, & friends; bought my sister Sapphires, and Diamonds, my mother Ruby and Diamonds, other friends gold, and some trinkets for me. I was having too much fun. Now I was running up these credit cards like I had money to pay them. (I didn't) I thought I would get a job to pay them but think about it. I was in my 20s, young, wild, and didn't know if I'd get the chance to travel like this again; so, I felt compelled to make the most of it and worry about the consequences later. It was my adventure and I loved it. I'm not one of these people who live life from the sidelines. Playing it nice and easy. Like Tina Turner says, "I don't do anything nice and easy, I do it nice and rough". Many people go through life, always saying if they had done this or if only I had done that. Well, I will have no regrets. I'd rather 'wear out than rust out'. I want to get all there is from life and then some. Suck the marrow out of the bones of life. We only pass this way once. When I close my eyes for the last time, then I can exhale. In the meantime, Life is to be lived.

I packed my jewels in my bag and after a week left for the airport. On the way, I passed a jewelry store with a beautiful Diamond Necklace in the window and I felt my mother should have it. So, I had the driver stop. I floated in like Claude Rains, thinking of him in the great 1946 film with Betty Davis called **Deception**, and I said, I'll take this, please. Here I go again; I had been called by a few shopkeepers 'the rich American'. I was spending money like candy or like I was rich and white. Well, they wrapped it nicely for me, put it in a lovely bag. I think it was only a thousand dollars, which would have been worth five times that in the states. Which was the reason rich Americans went there at that time to shop.

I said, "hurry please, I have a plane to catch." (Later, I was very sorry I said that.) I tucked the box under my arm, and we went to the airport. I'm walking through the airport and I saw several men coming straight at me. I said, "oh shit!" (how original). The leader said to come with me. I followed them to what looked like an interrogation room. They told me, Diners Club had declined my card and the Jewelry story demanded the Necklace back. I went into high drama mode.

I stood up and gave my best Sydney Poitier Impression. "Do you know who I am? How dare you! They Call Me Mr. Eames," aka (They call Me Mr. Tibbs). I have never been so humiliated. Bring me your superiors. They had no idea what I was talking about, so it was a wasted performance. Anyway, they told me I could not leave the country until they got the jewels back or the credit card company would accept the charges. I told them, in no uncertain terms, I sent my bags ahead of me, and the card would be responsible for the payment of this necklace. Now in those countries, this was 1977 the planes didn't leave every hour as they do now. And if I had missed that plane, I would be in that country another 2 or 3 days, until another flight was heading out of there.

The plane was leaving in about 30 minutes, and I was trying to bluff my way out of this mess. (I was really afraid that they would search my bag and find all of the diamonds I bought and confiscate all of them.) Since they didn't buy my performance, although I thought it was quite convincing, But then I'm partial. They were not having it. Sydney Poitier or not. I threw up my hands, and said, this is an outrage. Let me search my luggage just in case it wasn't in the bags I sent ahead of me. And I'll have my lawyers contact the embassy and file a formal complaint. I went through my luggage and 'Voila' Here I found it, I'm so sorry for this confusion. Please take this necklace and I'll have my lawyers deal with it later, I must leave now.

Once they got necklace I was free to leave with the bag of jewels I had in my suitcase. All was well. I'm sure to some, this shows a negative side to my character; but, like the 1934 hit song written by one of my favorite tortured souls the wonderfully witty Oscar Levant, **"Blame It on My Youth"**. And besides, had I not led this life, there wouldn't be anything exciting to write about. Again, I don't believe in sitting on the sidelines watching other people's adventures. I was creating my own. It's more fun that way. Try it. I believe in being thrown 'Smack Dab in The Middle 'of life. Yes, I've done it again, I've referenced another song because I'm full of song, It's always a song in my heart, and often something will lead me to a reference like **"Smack Dab In The Middle"**, which was written by one of the most important people in music, Jesse Stone, 1901-1999, also known by Charles "Chuck" Calhoun. I recorded one of his songs that he wrote, on my second CD (1996). "Shake Rattle and Roll.", which was a hit for Big Joe Turner in 1954. Many people recorded his music: Ray Charles, LeVern Baker, Louis Jordan, and countless others. Count Basie wrote in his autobiography that Jesse was the best pianist in Kansas City. The Great Ahmet Ertegun of Atlantic Records said Stone did more to develop the Rock and Roll sound than anybody else. He covered the gamut of music: Jazz/Blues/ Rock and Roll, and Pop. The last leg of my trip was Paris. *What a grand city.*

Wow. I see why Cole Porter wrote "I Love Paris" in 1953, the year I was born.

My good friend Patrick & 2 lovely ladies - Paris 1977

I was living on credit cards because I was going from country to country. Every country I went to I'd go to the Credit card office and got a few hundred in cash. This time I could only get a small amount.

I paid the Hotel up front with the credit card so that was covered. I was staying at The InterContinental Hotel. I went shopping on the Avenue des Champs-Elysees. Some say the most famous street in all of Europe. I saw the most beautiful Alligator shoes. Oh my God, I had to have them. They were exquisite. They were $500.00 and I gave the clerk my card, and he called the credit card company and they told him to cut the card in half now. Right now. Just start cutting. Don't stop until it's nothing left to cut. I was stunned. Not so much that my card was cut in tiny pieces, but that I didn't get those shoes. Now I understand Carrie Bradshaw. One of my favorite films is *The Bad Seed* 1956 staring Patty McCormack and Nancy Kelly, among other great cast members. But the scene when Rhoda screams, "Leroy give my shoes!" to the great character actor Henry Jones, was a great moment in film. My mother and I always referenced it and had a good laugh. However, I have digressed again. I was on the last leg of my trip, little money, no more working credit cards, the rest had been taken or was over the limit, and I was f----d. Luckily I had paid my Hotel and had some cash, but very little, and had another 7 days to stay in Paris. I walked to the garden across from the Hotel and this Frenchman saw me looking like the 1940 Rogers and Hart Classic song **"Bewitched, Bothered and Bewildered"**. *Have you heard Ella sing this? You should.*

He said are you American, I said yes, and we struck up a conversation, He, in broken English but better than my non-French. Like many Europeans, he was happy to meet a Black American. I have found it's an entirely different feeling from Europeans towards Black Americans In Europe. We hung out all of that day had lunch; and I told him I had to leave the hotel tomorrow, and did he know of a cheap place I could stay for about 7 days until my flight left for New York.

My father's retirement from banking 1981-The Eames family - Me, Marvin, Nedra, Father, Cookie, Kirk, Louis Jr.

He said, sure stay with me. I have a small apartment, but you can stay on the sofa. That was wonderful news. We packed my stuff and went to his small apartment on Rue Broca.(God is truly in the blessing business). I have always had Guardian Angels. I still do. I'm blessed. My karma is good. My heart is good. Good things always happen to me. Always. All of my life and in my past life. And it will happen in my next life. Of this, I'm certain.

I make mistakes and do some things I shouldn't, like spending money on credit cards. I'm human, but when one looks at the big picture, I believe, no I know, that God knows my core, my inner-ness. And it's good. At this writing, I'm 66 years old and I can say I have never purposely or intentionally done anything underhanded or wrong to anyone, ever. I don't speak ill of anyone, I don't gossip, I don't engage in anything negative. I know that's one of the reasons that everything works for good in my life. Drinking made me do foolish things, but that was the disease, not the real me.

We made our way to his apartment. I felt at home. Patrick was my first 'French friend', with a lovely and small French apartment. What a good time it was. I learned from meeting him that one has to hang out with a native Parisian to really see Paris, as in any country. I also learned later in my years, traveling and getting older and wiser, that the mistake I made then was to stay only at big American Hotels with other Americans, how boring is that. I could have stayed in America. (But I was in my 20s, that's all I knew) As Maya Angelou says, "If we knew better, we would do better".

There were only Americans or other tourists, everywhere I went in those big Hotels. However, meeting Patrick, now this was my first taste of real Europe with a native, eating in local dives, learning the language, the culture. It was just perfect. Patrick was maybe 28. He also said I was a rich American to him. (Which he reminded me of this past year when we spoke, 42 years later. I went to visit him in 2007 and we had a great time over a seafood dinner, in his beautiful and lovely countryside home in Cognac France.)

You see Patrick is very successful today. I'm so proud and happy for him. Like I said earlier, I keep "real" friends for a lifetime. It takes being a friend to have a friend. It was Patrick who introduced me to champagne and cognac. I had never had either, Where I'm from in Baton Rouge La, we drank Swiss Up, Bali Hi, Thunderbird, and Tokay. Just about all of those could be had for 69 cents a gallon, when I was growing up. And if you remember my saying earlier, I had stopped drinking in high school because I had gotten so drunk on beer and cheap wine, that I swore I would not do that again for all the gold/diamonds in South Africa.

But in Paris, it was different. It was intoxicating. We had the best champagne and lots of it. The best Cognac and lots of it. Paris is where my drinking started in earnest. The first night I had champagne, I drank an entire bottle, I acquired a taste for it from the first sip. The next night I tried Cognac for the first time and drank almost an entire bottle of. I have an addictive nature. It was the beginning of my total descent into madness.

I will never be able to thank Patrick for saving my life that summer day over 40 years ago. I was in Paris and had nowhere to go and he took me in.

I finally got back to America after traveling for over 13 weeks. It was good to be home. There truly is no place like home. I hated traveling like that for 13 weeks; and as a dumb American, I took too many clothes which I didn't need, and too many suitcases. Today when I travel I take one bag. But we learn as we get older what's important. Reminds me of the lovely Sammy Cahn/ J. Van Heusen song, (1961) **"The Second Time Around."** The line in the song which goes "Makes you think perhaps, that Love like youth is wasted on the young"

I was flat broke when I stepped off the plane at JFK Airport. No job and bills up to my ass. (Not much has changed at the writing of this book, and it's 2019). Any who... I was biking in Central Park ruminating about my long trip and glad to be home in New York and this guy was sitting on a bench writing, and me being, well me, said, "hi, what are you writing?" He said a song. I told him I was a singer and we started talking and I told him I had just gotten back from traveling, and how annoying it was with all the luggage I had. Remember, folks, this was the late 1970s, and ' everybody who's anybody ' had to have Gucci, Pucci, 'hoochie', Pierre Cardin, Mark Cross, YSL, or some designer name on the luggage. So, I had the entire Gucci set of luggage. I was the typical young American thinking I was living large, traveling the world and dragging a set of Gucci bags behind me. Today I shop at the 99-cent store and love it. Don who was sitting on the park bench writing, and whom I had just met and had this conversation with told me, "you didn't have to carry the bags." I said, "excuse me?" He repeated it again. So, I said, "yes I did, how else would they get to where I'm going?" He said you made that choice to carry them, you didn't have to do it. You could have left them. This went back and forward until we both just gave up and called a truce. Drove me nuts.

Over time, Don and I became best friends. I am so blessed to have met and befriended him. He changed my life. I needed a job and he worked as a waiter and brought me into his place where he worked and taught me the ropes. I knew nothing about being a waiter. Donald Basford was a very smart 'WASP'. His father worked in some capacity on the Atom Bomb and his mother was a painter/artist. Don taught me so much. He was 6 years older than me and very well educated and booked-learned. And because his mother was an artist, he knew the world of art like nobody else I had ever met before. I had never gone to the museum and lived right next door to one of the biggest and most famous in the world, the Metropolitan. (I'd gone to grand parties there but not for anything as cultural as actually seeing the exhibits.) *Can you imagine?*

Don said, "let's go, let me show you the museum." So off we went. I was excited, just watching his excitement. I love to learn as much as I can from anyone willing to teach. He could look at a painting and know if it's a Rembrandt, Picasso, Vermeer, Degas, Homer, Van Gogh, etc. He could tell you the certain brush strokes which were used, what kind of paint. He was amazing. We would spend hours in the Frick Museum. A private collection of art from the Henry Clay Frick family located on Fifth Ave and 70th St. A grand mansion built-in 1913. He would also tell me how the sister still lived up the stairs in this grand museum, at that time.

And that it was the home of three 'Vermeer's' that were privately owned. He was so full of knowledge and I'm blessed he imparted it with me. He introduced me to Chopin, Liszt, Rachmaninoff, Brahms, Tchaikovsky, Horowitz, the Opera. That was his world. And what a wonderful world it was. Again, I'm so blessed he shared his knowledge and friendship with me. He also knew I was eager to learn and grow. I had ambition and he saw it and encouraged it.

He told me things he thought I would need. He insisted I read Tolstoy, Dostoevsky, Henry Miller, Updike, Hemmingway, Emerson, Thoreau, and many more. *What a brilliant man.* I cherished his friendship, I learned so much from him; and according to him, he learned so much from me. He opened up his world to me, and I opened up my world to him. I introduced him to Oscar Peterson, Sarah Vaughn, Count Basie, Charlie Parker, Coltrane, Errol Garner, Nancy Wilson, Ella and Lady Day. He read my books of James Baldwin, Ralph Ellison, Richard Wright, Du Bois, James Weldon Johnson, Malcolm, Carter G Woodson, Fredrick Douglass, etc. I introduced him to Louisiana Gumbo and Catfish.

It was a deep and real friendship. I began drinking Cognac by the bottles from the time I got back to New York, It's been said that some people have a gene which is predisposed to alcoholism. If it exists, I had it. From the first drink, I couldn't stop. But I was handsome, witty, charming, world-traveled, well-read, the life of the party. But I was slowly spiraling out of control and didn't see it coming. Don got me a job as a waiter and it went well, but the alcohol always got me fired, sooner or later. As I said earlier, I have been fired from every job I have had since 1969. I went through a few dozen waiter jobs, drinking like a fish and taking pills and cocaine. But everybody else was the problem never me. They were the stupid ones. I gave up the pills and substituted it with Booze. During this time, I was hanging out at studio 54, and Xenon's. The Discos of that era.

I delved more and more into drugs/alcohol. Living the fast life. Pimps, hookers, drugs, parties day and night , the Palladium, the Playboy Club, Smalls Paradise in Harlem , Mikel's, Peter Browns, Russ Browns, Angry Squire, Trudy Heller's, the 5 Spot, Birdland, Village Gate, Marty's, Maxwell Plums, the Copacabana on 60th St. off 5th Ave, Regine's, Sweetwater's and many more I'm sure I have forgotten. Still singing every chance I got at open mic and jam sessions. Night after night after night for years. I would get off work and run to the jam session and sit in, it was real dues paying. It was my passion. Drugs and music. I was with Don one night when I was working at a coffee shop on 86th Street and Lexington Ave, owned by Augie Ray. Don came to have coffee and would sit and write in little note pads often, and for hours almost daily. It was a real passion.

He lived in the area on East 92nd St. off Second Ave, I hope to have some of his writings published someday. (It's sad that because Don had black friends, his racist neighbors in the area threatened him and beat him and warned him never to a bring black person around this area.. So, he had to give up his apartment and move in with me for a while until he got another place). Sick people indeed. Don suggested we go see a swinging pianist/singer at Rupert's Towers on 3rd Avenue in the 90s. So, after work, we went and had a few drinks. As usual, I had more drinks than anybody there. But that night it was a lovely European girl sitting at the table enjoying this very good pianist named Louis Hancock who became my best friend, until his death around 2002. She and I made eyes and flirted with each other the entire night. I will call her D. She now lives in Palm Beach and is a grandma. We spoke this week and she invited me to Palm Beach to lay in the sun this winter in 2019, as I'm trying to finish this book.

She sent me a drink, I sent her a drink, and I joined her table. By that time my drink of choice was Vodka. This lovely young lady and I made plans to meet the next night. We went out to dinner and to see a show. We walked back to my apartment and made love all night.

This French gal did some things to me, I still get warm even now, if I think too long. We dated for a while, maybe a year or so, but my drinking, as usual, ruined it like it did most things in my life, and I hadn't realized it until a long time later. We are still very close after all these years. She was very special in my life at a time when I needed her. I took her to Baton Rouge to meet my family. We enjoyed each other's company. But the alcohol was becoming more and more the focus of my world. I was becoming intolerable and unbearable.

I have always been searching for something and couldn't stand to be tied down to anybody. I still can't. So, I drank. Got fired and drank some more, cursed everybody out and drank more, but because I was charming and affable until I went off, I always somehow managed to get jobs to keep me going until I had one drink too many and turned tables over, fighting, cursing and screaming, in a rage. I was completely out of control. It happened more times than I can tell you. I met a White guy at the bar in the **Playboy Club**. We got drunk and he told me his wife liked Black men. She was White. So, I knew where this was leading. We had a few more drinks, to cut to the chase, they became my meal ticket for a while. Which was so helpful because I couldn't keep a job, and needed money, If I f--k-d her once a week, my rent and other bills got paid. I needed my rent paid, she needed, even craved 'Black sex'. End of story, slow curtain, fade to black. The end. We do what we have to do to survive.

There were lots of that going on in the Playboy Club, Plato's Retreat (The owner Larry Levinson went to prison for tax evasion in 1981).

Everybody was swinging. I F--d her so good one night, 'visions of sugar plums danced in her head'. I've been with men and women on several continents. 'Ménage a trois' was common as mud. What boggles my mind is why would anyone care? I can care less what you are doing. In fact, the lady I speak of, her photo is still on my wall in the Gold room and people who come to Parlor Jazz at my home ask, 'who is this?' I say, "a friend." Which she and her husband became. It was swinging times indeed.

More love less war!

Now, this kind of behavior may be shocking to some, frowned upon by others, but in reality, it is very common. Just not talked about in 'polite society'. It's been going on since the beginning of American history in this country. And let's not get into how long the Europeans have been perverted. I find it so hypocritical, the outrage over this kind of 'activity'. .Grow up, who gives a F—k! More people should have more sex more times a day, more often, with whomever floats your boat. If legal. Because one day you will wake up dead and the party will be over. And I can hear some say, I should've done this or done that, or (if 'I-da' done this or if I -da' done that).

In fact, one of the greatest men on earth lived a similar existence in the 1940s as I was leading during this time. Sex, and drugs, players, pimps, hookers, alcohol. That 'fast life' that we all know exist, and many secretly lust for, but few have the nerve to taste it, smell it, to wallow in it. Remember, Throw me 'smack dab in the middle', every time.

Malcolm was paid to procure, to perform sex acts, to pleasure White women in front of rich White men, who wouldn't or couldn't pleasure their wives, until their weird sexual **Mandingo fantasies** had subsided. This scenario was also played out the other way with Black women. And vice versa. It was usually perverted, and it still goes on today. Even more so due to the internet. Interracial sexual taboos exist. It's as American as apple pie. This great man I'm referring to talked about this part of his sordid past in one of the most remarkable books written, **The Autobiography of Malcolm X.**

I won't shrink from my past either. We don't judge a man from where he starts, but from where he finishes.

Americans need to grow up sexually. I will never understand for the life of me why a politician gets fired and runs out of town for sleeping with someone other than his wife. As long as he's doing his job why should you care? If he and his wife can work through it, what business is it of yours to destroy a man or woman for something as normal as sex? People are killing people, robbing, stepping over the homeless, terrorist, ignoring the mentally ill, world hunger, unemployment, illiteracy, racism, doing all kinds of horrible stuff, but God forbid if two people have sex and make love, or make hate… whatever works. Then everybody is enraged, calling for their heads on a gold platter. Why does America seem to have this need to destroy each other over silliness? Then put them on every TV show to sell a book about it.

I'm just asking.

Edmund Burke said **"To make us love our country, our country ought to be lovely"**.

Their money for my' sexual favors' allowed me time to work more on my music. Later I joined the great jazz pianist Barry Harris workshop, The Jazz Cultural Theater. What a wonderful place. I made good friends, there are many of whom I have today, singer Linda Raye, Thomas Hilton, pianist Alan Kaman who was "responsible for me getting my TV show years later", Jazz pianist

Rodney Kendrick, a wonderful pianist who is married to the daughter of Diana Ross/Barry Gordy, Rhonda, a very good actress and vocalist. She is also the founder of Ross Realty Int'l. There were many more musicians I met there.

Those were great times. I'd sing there often with other struggling musicians trying to hone our craft. Thank you, Barry. Another place I joined was Cobi Narita's UJC, Universal Jazz Coalition. Where I got to work with one of the best trios, Harold Mabern, the swinging Memphis pianist, bassist Jamil Nassar, and drummer Frank Gant. Cobi would bring in great vocalists like Abby Lincoln, Dakota Staton, to listen to us and give pointers.

In 2019, Cobi still has a wonderful jazz workshop on West 73rd St. in NYC on Fridays with the legendary pianist Frank Owens, who has worked with many of the great singers from Lena Horne, Johnny Mathis, and many others, plus musical director for Broadway shows, *Ellington's, Sophisticated Ladies,* and *Ain't Misbehavin.* He was the first musical director for the David Letterman Show, and a grand gentleman. I love him and am so honored to have worked with him.

 Once during this period, I went to see Lou Rawls at a club; and to me, he's one of the best ever. After the show, I went to talk to him and I asked him, like the young fan that I was, "do you have any advice for an up and coming singer?", He looked at me and in his very deep voice said "pay your dues", and walked off. I was shocked at that time, but years later, I realized he was 100 % correct. In this business, it's the only way to last.

I was so grateful to have this experience. Working on stage live with masterful musicians, I ended up doing several shows with Harold Mabern, and Jamil. To this day I'm grateful to them for being there for me when I wasn't vocally ready yet. When Harold wasn't working he would make my gigs for the little money I could pay him. It's musicians like that who reach back and extend a hand to the younger and up and coming musicians who will carry this torch. There were a few other jazz workshops in the late 70s and early 80s that I hung out in. The hip singer and friend, Joe Lee Wilson had a hot spot in the East Village called the Ladies Fort, and there was/is a jazz mobile, which Billy Taylor headed.

I had one of my first professional gigs at a place called Jason's Park Royal on West 73rd St. Off Central Park West in a Hotel. Dawn Hampton was holding court there during that time, the sister of trombonist Slide Hampton and sister Paula Hampton. I have always been one to preserve my life and I recorded that first show in 1981. I just heard it recently and it's not bad for a live recording. My very first recording. I plan to have it re-mastered for the archives.

I worked with a wonderful pianist Burt Eckhoff, and don't remember the bassist. I was so drunk I went to sit on my stool and the stool fell off the stage. My mother flew up from Baton Rouge, Louisiana, and my sister, her husband, and another friend all came out to support me, and we had a nice crowd. My father was in a meeting in Baton Rouge and came up a few days later so he missed that show.

The 1970s

My first Professional Show in NYC, 1981

JaRon @ Dangerfields early 1980's

My parents have always supported everything and anything I did, and for that I'm grateful. I wasn't pleasant when I drank; people think they are, but they are not. Not when one drank as much as I did. I could be a nasty drunk, with a smile. Sarcastic. I would start out nice and polite, the life of the party, full of witticism, grand stories about my trips abroad, then in a flash, I'd go off. Completely off. Right into the deep water. I had become in the flash of an eye, Jekyll, and Hyde. When provoked, the meanness oozed out of me mellifluously. Like puss. And the alcohol exacerbated it. I wanted something, I wanted stardom. I was chasing it.

'Thoreau' said about happiness, "Happiness is like a butterfly, the more you chase it, the more it will elude you, but if you turn your attention to other things, it will come and sit softly on your shoulders".

It took me a long time to learn that. I thought because I had traveled the world and wined and dined with famous people, and lived in this fast and exciting life, that I was entitled to be treated special. Oh, I was special all right, but not for the reasons the alcohol/drugs had me imagine. I was slowly becoming a monster. I was drinking a fifth of vodka a night. Straight, no chaser. Which turned into a half gallon a night.

Ice cold, right out of the freezer. I started out only drinking the top-shelf Vodka, you know the names, but towards the end of my madness, I was drinking the cheapest vodka I could fine, in the big bottle. It had gotten so bad; I couldn't even make it to my mailbox without a drink. I slept with the bottle in my bed. Before I got out of bed I had the bottle up to my mouth to pick me up. The bottle was my constant companion. I needed no one else. How sad is that? I was drinking myself into a delusional abyss.

Once a friend the pianist Louis Hancock, came to visit and I took out the trash, I had 2 hefty trash bags full of only half gallon vodka bottles. He reminded me of that years later. I had one of my famous dinner parties. I love to entertain, that's how I grew up. One such party I remember I had 4-6 friends over for a small dinner, I prepared a Louisiana dish, and all was going well. When one friend either said something or moved the saltshaker, or drank water, or was simply just breathing, it didn't matter, but it set me off. A particularly violent episode. I stood up from the dinner table, under my magnificent chandelier, beautifully set china, turned the table over, went in the back of my apartment, came out in a mink coat, underneath it I was completely naked with a hammer in my hand above my head, and ran everybody out of my apartment. It was awful. Deep rages, screaming and ranting to the top of my lungs.

Episodes like this one began to happen on a regular basis. Wherever I went. If I stayed long enough, something was bound to happen, and it wasn't pretty. It had gotten to the point people would see me coming and cross the street, saying, oh God, there he is. People stopped inviting me places or if they did, they would hide the liquor; but by that time, I had taken to carrying a flask wherever I went, even on my bike which I rode often, as I do to this day. I never went out of my apartment without a container of vodka on me. I drank around the clock. All-day every day.

I got a few more gigs during this time at clubs like Sweet Waters, The Angry Squire, where one night the sound system was awful and in a fit, I threw the microphone to the floor, and I think to this day the great bassist Jamil Nassar is still upset with me over that, and I don't blame him. (I'm sorry Jamil.) I also was hired at the famous **Smalls Paradise**. I was hired by the brother of Dakota Staton, Fred Staton, the wonderful saxophonist who was the owner of Smalls during the time. (Fred and I worked together many times, and on Valentine's Day 2007at the nursing home where Dakota has been for the last few years we had a show which I'll post on YouTube.) He's was a good man and I'm so blessed to have known him. He passed in 2017 at 102 years young. Playing to the very end and playing well.

Working at Smalls was a real treat, the famous Harlem jazz joint. All of the legendary jazz giants who worked on that stage. What a blessing. My parents came up from Baton Rouge as they often did when I had any kind of important performance. It's support and love like that, which makes one able to climb any hurdle and move mountains. They were pleased with my performance. It was all about paying dues. I wasn't really ready nor seasoned, but I did well. And of course, I was drunk. I have not worked in Harlem since that show at Smalls almost 40 years ago. Once I closed the show for George Kirby at **Rodney Dangerfield's**. It was a good show and Mr. Dangerfield was pleased. I was asked back. I liked him a lot.

Chapter 4

The 1980s:
The End of Drinking Was Close

S till going nightly to jam sessions and picking up gigs here and there was my life. I got a job as a waiter at Buddy Rich's club in Midtown, called Buddy's place, Mr. Rich was one of the greatest drummers in jazz. And he had a temper.

Linda Raye and Me at the Sheraton Russell Hotel on Park 1985 Singing Baby It's Cold Outside (Benny Green on Piano)

One night Buddy was playing the drums and I was drunk, someone bumped me, I believe on purpose, and I dropped a very large tray of glasses that shattered them in the middle of his solo, Buddy had me fired that night. I started having DTs 'delirium tremens', I'd awake screaming, "It's spiders, get them off me", and swatting them away. I had many of those nights.. Very frightening, deeply disturbing. It was like the wonderfully brilliant 1957 movie starting Joanne Woodward, *Three Faces of Eve.* It's like I had multiple personality disorder. But hell, if one drinks a bottle of straight vodka nightly, one should expect a little madness, wouldn't you think?

But most times in public I was my normal funny, happy self, up to a point, until somebody would do something to set me off. But more times than not, I think I would have imagined a perceived slight, and off I went. My good 'friend' was the coke man. I got it free or for very little money, so I was drinking a bottle of vodka a night and a few grams of coke, the blackouts started coming more and more frequently.

The alcohol had me in a coma-like state and the coke had me speeding. I had left the Dolls alone; they didn't mix well with booze the way I was drinking. I would black out/ not pass out, but blackout, and yet I'm still up and speeding, walking, talking, but not aware of what you are doing. Your brain has shut off, but you can function. The medical term is called Anterograde Amnesia. It's caused from alcoholic intoxication. It affects the short-term memory, not the long-term memory. (This very day I cannot remember something that happened 5 minutes ago, but something years ago, is fresh as day.

Sometimes, I did not remember the days of what I had done, or where I had been. Some nights I'd crawl home beat up and not know how it happened. The first thing I'd do is get a drink. I worked in night clubs as a waiter so I was around liquor and would leave work at 4am and head to after hour clubs in Harlem and drink until it was time to go back to work the next night. One of my dear friends to this day.

The 1980s: The End of Drinking Was Close

I'll call her Ronica, who used to be a manager of a seafood restaurant on Madison Ave. was in that circle where this went on. She's doing fine now also, thank God.

We worked at Jewels, a Black Juke joint on 68th St. and 1st Ave. A hell of a joint, I loved it. I'd wait tables with 9 plates on a big tray and a glass of vodka in my other hand to keep me calm. Never wasted a drop. Another good friend worked with me who didn't drink or do drugs - a good woman. I'll call her Bert; she and I are still good friends today and talk on the phone often. I got fired from Jewels for my usual madness, fighting, threatening to cut somebody's throat. God had to be watching over me. My friend Bert asked me one night in Jewels, how are you going to cut so and so's throat and you don't have a knife? But alcohol makes one talk like that in the moment of a rage. So as usual, I'm out of work again, and took a job as a messenger part time.

This was my life, I was drinking now a half gallon of vodka a night, I know how much I drank because every night at 9:50pm, I'd have to run to 87th St. and Second Ave to the liquor store to get another half-gallon of vodka.(they closed at 10 pm) and I live on 85th St. They would have the bottle waiting for me on the counter. It went on like this night after night for a long, long time until one night I was found sitting in a pothole/puddle of water in the middle of Manhattan in nothing but my underwear, screaming and ranting that I was a 'movie star'. I was looking around for Mr. Demille. I was finally ready for my close-up.

Authentic madness had set in. The ambulance pulled up and out came 2 people carrying the white strait jacket, for me. This time I had truly stepped into the twilight zone, with a one-way ticket. My worst and most secret nightmare had come true. Insanity runs in my blood. My older brother died in an insane asylum. They strapped me in good and tight. I was in rare form that night, screaming and cussing up a storm, saying that I was too important to be treated like this, and did they know who my father was, better yet did they know who I was? On and on and on I went. I really gave a grand performance that night, at the top of my voice .My eyes would glass over and became empty, soulless, humanless. I ranted on like this for quite a while.

They took me to the mental ward of Roosevelt Hospital in Manhattan's Westside. Once there, they tried to talk to me to calm me down by asking me many questions . Finally, they shot me full of Thorazine. It was a very big needle and lots of juice (that's what they give Schizophrenic patients /Mental patients) and I qualified. They were asking me all kinds of questions, about who to contact where I lived, has this ever happened before? And in my maddens, I was rattling off phone numbers, one which was my apartment phone number. I had gotten Don a job at Jewels, and he was still working at this time. He was off work this night.

Don had keys to my apartment but nobody, and I mean nobody ever answers my phone, even today, if someone is calling my house they are calling for me. Nobody else. Any-who, that night he stopped by to get some of his writings. The doctors called my apartment and he picked up the phone. When he answered hello, he told me later that he heard me screaming in the background and Don knew years earlier I had a major problem which is the reason he pulled away from me as most did. He knew this night was coming , and it had now arrived. In full throttle.

When the city finds you like they found me, naked and deranged in the middle of the Manhattan, screaming that 'I'm a movie star', they don't let you go on your own, someone has to sign you out. Don was on his way. Thank God he answered my phone. (God works in mysterious ways is surely true in this case, as in most of my life.) As it's said, God may not be there when you want him, but when you need him he's always on time.

If Don had not answered my phone, I would have been locked up in the mental ward for who knows how long, shot full of powerful medicines, and this may have all turned out very differently. Once they get you in those places, they have a way to make you even more nuts by keeping you doped up with very powerful drugs, 10 times stronger than what I had been taking all of my life.

When Don got out of the taxi, he told me later, that he could hear me on the street 5 stories below through the open window, still screaming and ranting . When he got to the floor, the Thorazine had taken effect and I was calm as a lamb.

They unhooked me from the straight jacked and Don took me home. The doctors said if I didn't stop drinking I'd die; my liver was extremely enlarged. I slept 2-3 days. I cried and promised myself I would stop drinking. At least for a while. The hardest thing for a drunk is the mere idea of never having a drink again. It's just unthinkable. That word 'Never'. I did good. I lasted about 5 days, and by that time was not only climbing the walls, but my DT's were bad, very bad.

When I did pick up the bottle again, I drank enough to make up for the 5 days without . I just didn't want to stop. I loved vodka. Believe it or not, I loved the way it made me feel. I loved everything about it. However, I was "Beginning to See the Light" as Ellington, Harry James, Johnny Hodges and Don George wrote in 1944.

Nothing seemed to be able to get me to stop drinking, one would think being in a straitjacket would do the trick. But delusions of grandeur had taken over completely. "When one is seeking answers, one must quiet the soul to hear them." I was seeking answers.

I drank and did coke for a while longer, until one-night Sarah Vaughn came to the Blue Note in New York (1985). It was New Year's Eve going into 1985. I had been singing at the Blue Note jam sessions on and off for a while, and the wonderful trumpeter Ted Curson was the host of the late-night jams.

This particular night was a night to remember. High rollers, a very happening audience. Sarah Vaughn, (one of the greatest voices in American popular music) and her band. It was a packed house. What a night.

Now I had always said to God, 'God, if you give me the right room, the right band, the right audience, I'll show the world what I can do.' Wouldn't you know it. As always when I ask God for things, I get them.

After Sarah Vaughn finished her swinging show, Ted Curson said to the audience, we have a special guest who is going to lead off jam session, JaRon Eames. I took the mike and said hello, etc. We did the 1931 hit song written by Simon and Marks, "All of Me". I drank a bottle of vodka and did a few lines of coke.

Everything I had asked God for; He gave me that night at the Blue Note. The house band struck up the opening note and damn near blew me off the stage. I was so high so totally f----d up, that I was only a shell of myself. My voice was so weak, it was pitiful. I got through it because I'm still a professional, but in my opinion it was simply awful. I had a chance to show the world, and because of drugs and alcohol I blew it. Remember, you never get a second chance to make a first impression.

I took a girl singer I liked a lot, Linda Raye to the Blue Note that night. I left with my tail between my legs. In total humiliation. We got in a taxi and I turned to her and said, "that was my last drink," and so help me God, when I said that, a white halo came over my head and everything became real bright.

I'm sure you have heard this before, but it's true, a bright white halo surrounded me, like the heavens opened up and wrapped me in comfort. I felt peace. We went to another club, but I didn't want to stay. I needed to get home and call my family and tell them I was ready to stop drinking. They also knew I was completely out of control. The last time they saw me I was in Baton Rouge and I acted so ugly and raged so out of control. A cop pulled a gun on me in the airport because I had demanded that the airlines get me a private plane back to New York and out of this small backward town. I'm lucky to be alive, trust me. Here I was demanding a private plane and I think I had about 35 cents to my name.

Me & John Burr Bassist, Michael Wolff Piano- 1985
(My first show sober)

I left Linda at the Angry Squire and I came home. I was a complete mess, yet deliciously calm. I can't explain how calm I was. I called my family and told them I'd had my last drink. They didn't know what to make of it; but they were happy I was trying to make some changes.

My father said "son do you want us to come get you and bring you home? What do you want us to do?" I said, "I will be OK, I just wanted you to know that I'm never going to drink again." We said goodbye and I hung up. I was lying on the carpet floor and put my hand on the phone book which was lying on the floor next to me. I didn't see that it was there, it just happened to be there, and it was opened to AA. I didn't look for it, when my hand rested on that phone book, it just went to the AA page. I called the number and they said we have a meeting in about 30 min, right on the corner from my apartment. I went.

I only remember sitting in the back of this meeting, broken in spirit and soul and body and mind. I cried the entire time. Some old white guy, a very kind man I had no idea who he was sat next to me with his arms around me and held me while I sobbed. That was the beginning of my recovery and the regaining of my sanity. Thank you Ted Curson.

If you want to know what my drinking days were like, see the 1962 film, *The Days of Wine and Roses* with Jack Lemon and Lee Remick. It's my life in a nutshell.(I can't watch it without crying, to this day.) The scene of Lemon in the green house, wow. Probably the best film of the genre, that and 1945 classic 'The Lost Weekend' with Ray Milland. Or perhaps the great Susan Hayward film, *I'll Cry Tomorrow*(1955) the autobiography of singer/actress Lillian Roth, which was brilliant.

In fact Susan was nominated for an Oscar for her performance. For movies about drunks. These are three of the best.

Getting sober was hell. Those first few days/weeks without a drink, had me climbing the walls out of my mind. I chain-smoked and drank gallons of coffee like every other drunk in the AA meetings. In the beginning I went to meeting's daily. In fact, you have to if you want to stay sober. Sometimes I went to two meetings a day, morning and night. Most of that time I never said a word. I'd just sit there and listen to horror stories of other drunks who live the same madness I had in their own way. Thank God there's an Alcoholics Anonymous meeting every hour somewhere in New York.

I'll tell you two stories, which still stand out in my head. A young White guy, maybe in his late 20's early 30s had drank /drugged himself into AA. Once after meeting we went for coffee. In the conversation we wondered what makes people end up the way we had. Then he told me the most shocking story I have ever heard. As a kid growing up, his mother would make him perform oral sex on her, while his father penetrated him. I became physically ill.

I had nothing in my background that wasn't anything but perfect as far as I was concerned, so what was my reason for drinking a half gallon of vodka a day? I wanted to be a "star" was all I could think of, and it didn't turn out like I had hoped perhaps? However, I decided I just liked to drink, period. I don't think it always has to be some profound reason, And before you know it, the alcohol controls you and your life. To this day I still miss a cold glass of Vodka, but I know I can't have any ever again or I'll end up back in a straitjacket, or the morgue. The little man in my head does not know when to stop. Therefore, every time, I lose control. Total control. If only I could just have one or two drinks then stop, but with alcoholics, it's not possible. I'm an alcoholic.

I come from a long line of drinkers in my family. My father drank only Scotch, Cutty Sark, all his life. But he ran the Bank he helped start, never missed a day of work. My mom 'Cookie' drank, as well as my siblings. As I mentioned earlier, we had parties at my home every week, and liquor, good food, good people, and jazz flowed. Say amen, somebody.

But I seem to be the only one who had the alcoholic gene, which produces Alcoholic madness. To this day, I shutter at the thought of what that poor young man went through. Another story I remember was this older white man who talked about how he loved his wife and two daughters.

One night he was laying on the sofa, drinking and smoking, watching TV until he was drunk. His wife and 2 girls were asleep upstairs in the home, and he fell asleep, drunk, with a cigarette burning. He managed to escape. His family all burned to death. It's been said that a drunk must hit his or her bottom before they see the light. I'm grateful I hit mine before it was too late.

Drunks have many stories like this. The lucky/smart, blessed ones find a higher power and with the grace of God, this monster is slain. I'm blessed to still be here and tell my story. Maybe my story can save some other souls who are going through their own nightmarish situation.

One of the hardest parts for me was after my 90 days in AA, was when I had to stand in front of this group of strangers and "testify". (face the other drunks and tell my story.) Believe it or not, I'm a very private person and to this day, I think that was one the hardest things I have ever had to do. I can state categorically, AA saved my life and I have been sober, free of drugs and alcohol since New Year's Day 1985.

And for that I'm deeply grateful. It can be done if you really want to get sober. You have three choices, the mental ward,(been there, done that) death, or sobriety. It's up to you. You really can do it. I did. So did millions of others Don't think that you are alone. You are not, just reach out... help is waiting.

My first show sober, Girlfriend DM, Cookie- Daddy and Me (Angry Squire 1985)

After a few months into my sobriety, I wanted to get back on stage. I have been going to every show Nancy Wilson had in New York since 1973, so I Knew the band very well. At that time, it consisted of Pianist Michael Wolf, Bassist John B. Williams, and Drummer Roy McCurdy. So, me being, well, me, ran into Michael Wolf and said I was putting together a show at a small club called Angry Squire on 23rd At. and 7th Ave., and if he wasn't on the road with Nancy, I'd love for him to play on my gig. Now understand, Mike was used to the biggest gigs, the biggest and best rooms and real money. Working with Nancy Wilson, Cannonball Adderley, Sonny Rollins was big time. He said sure JaRon. I was overcome with joy. A real mensch. My friend Don was very proud that I had made it into sobriety. We got back to writing music together He became sick with cancer and had 2 bad years fighting this monster. He died from it in 1987. I was there for him until the end. Thank God I was sober, otherwise I don't think I would've been there. He was a truly special human being and played a major part in what I am today.

I will never forget it. To this day I'm deeply grateful for Michael's support by working with me. I had been sober for a few months and was so excited about working with Michael, and on bass was John Burr, I don't remember the drummer. Anyway, my parents flew up and the club was full. I knew I was in good hands, so the show had to be OK, regardless.

Jazz club where I performed often Badenscher Hof in Berlin 1990's - Reggie Moore Piano, Sherry Bertram Drums, Thomas Fassnau Bass.

When you have a top-notch rhythm section behind you, they can carry you up to a point. I did well, I was proud of myself. I was nowhere near ready vocally for such heavy weights I shared the stage with, but it sure was fun. And good dues- paying. Also, my family was very proud of me. My first show sober. My life sober was getting better, I was alive for the first time since I was a kid; and I was also working as a waiter in a nice seafood restaurant. Me and work of any kind other than my music or music related just annoyed me. I always felt like a fish out of water in 'normal jobs'. But I had to work, so I went from one job to the next. Picking up gigs when I could, and

The 1980s: The End of Drinking Was Close

happy to be alive. It went on like this, until one day I got a waiter job that I liked in a restaurant called Charlie O's in Shubert Alley in the theater district on West 45th St. I was in the thick of New York's Broadway. I started there in the middle of 1985 and soon found out that It was some of the worst and most nasty people I'd ever worked with, anywhere. (But I made great money, working just the diner shift 6pm-8pm.)

Most of the all-white wait staff didn't want me there, and I tried to ignore them. I really did. The host, an overweight white effeminate man, wouldn't seat my section like he sat the other waiters. This happens in all restaurants, but here It was just blatant .Because I wasn't in the 'click' I guess, but I had been through a lot in my life and didn't have time for this childishness. I was there simply to make money to pay bills and get on with my life. Many waiters are wanna-be show businesspeople and can be very vicious, mean and petty. Just for the sake of being vicious (I discovered this to be true about a lot of the people I met in LA. - completely plastic).

Even when I was drunk, people still liked me up to a point. I had several run-ins with the staff and once they understood I never acquired the taste for shit, they found it's best to leave me alone. They did. For a while. I don't like clicks, I'm my own click. I'm a party of 4. All by myself. Period . So, I had to fight to get tables. I was always the last to be seated. You know the saying, "last hired, first fired."

His name was Joe, I think, and he would seat the people in my section he thought wouldn't tip, Foreigners, Blacks, Latinos, Young Whites. (I always got great tips) Waiters make tips on personality. And like Lloyd Price used to sing, in 1959 "cause I got , personality, walk, personality, talk, personality," written by Harold Logan. He couldn't understand how I always made tips. He was stuck on the stereotypes as so many are. Poor thing.

This went on for about a year. They disliked me because I wasn't one to kiss ass and be 'grateful' to them as they thought I should have been to be 'allowed' to work there . But I had my eyes on the prize. What really drove them nuts is when the legendary Steve Allen brought his radio show into the restaurant to interview Broadway performers Live on Nation Wide Radio (WNEW). Mr. Allen was, among other things, the original host of the "Tonight Show" before Johnny Carson , or Jack Parr. And he has written over 14,000 songs. One of the most, if not the most famous, was *This Could Be the Start of Something Big* (1956). He was hosting a radio show from Charlie O's restaurant bringing the legends of Broadway, and Cabaret, night clubs, comedy, etc. I was supposed to be serving lunch with the rest of the waiters and when they came out of the kitchen carrying trays of food, and baskets of bread, there I am sitting on my bar stool next to the grand piano holding court. Singing. the song *is You,* the Jerome Kern/Oscar Hammerstein 1932 classic. They looked as if they wanted to horse whip me. One of the waiters who was also a performer said to one of the co-workers that It was selfish of me. I replied "In my case self-absorption is completely justified. I have never discovered any other subject quite so worthy of my attention".

Now, if you think I was going to pass up that chance, then you have surely taken leave of your senses. Steve Allen wasn't much of a talker when he wasn't 'On'. When he would come to the restaurant he would have onion soup and go over the show. I tried to make conversation when management wasn't looking because we weren't supposed to 'bother' him. But me, being well, me, thought that was just too silly for words, and made it a point to have something to say to him whenever I could. So, when some guest was late I approached him and said something to the fact, "Mr. Allen, you should let me sing a song until the guest arrives." He did. It was a major success; it went over very well. I was delighted, and several people including many friends heard it because it was broadcast live on WNEW the big station for this kind of music. Don was in the hospital and he heard it and loved it.

Well that did it. Management and staff all wanted to teach me a lesson. *Who did I think I was?* I was there to serve as a waiter. Period. They were furious with me. (It still makes me laugh today.) But little did they know I had been in battle for years and had a hide like an old rhino.

As Mommy Dearest said, "This ain't my first time at the rodeo." They came after me from all sides, after that. They wanted me out.

'Those who dare to dream must be prepared to be laughed at and condemned. Chances are the people closest to you will accuse you of arrogance. I have always found it strange when people go out of their way to belittle someone's dream. I want everybody to get just what they want out of life. I don't know any other way to be. I will always do whatever I can to help someone reach their goals. But to try and stop someone? To block someone? People, don't you understand you get back what you put out?

I had a chance to sing on Live Radio. Why should I give that up? Would you?

Everything they tried backfired. "Envy makes a person ugly." They even accused me of stealing and fired me. Of course, they had no basis in fact for this, but this young cocky Italian manager took the side of the young White workers and that was that. Or so they thought. I was told to go home. To leave the restaurant. I left the restaurant, went home, dressed in one of my many suits I had bought in Rome and went to the head office of the owner of the largest independently- owned restaurants in New York, the Reese organization Dennis and Irving Reese.

They own most of the chain places, too many to list here. Roy Rogers, Pizza Hut, Steak N Brew, KFC, TGI Fridays, Dunkin Donuts and many more. They also owned the Charlie O's chain. So, I show up unannounced at his office, and his secretary curtly told me I couldn't see Mr. Reese because he was a very busy man, that I had no appointment, and went back to doing whatever she was doing as though I wasn't there. So, I looked at her for about a minute so she could see who she was dealing with. I'm not that easily dismissed by anybody. I said to her my business is important, I'll wait.

So, as God would have It, after a few a short minutes, Mr. Reese comes out to get some papers off of her desk. I stood up with my hand stretched out to shake his hand, introducing myself.

I said, "Mr. Reese, my name is JaRon Eames and I work at your restaurant in Shubert Alley. The manager is stealing your money and I can prove it." Well, this secretary from the Bronx with too much make -up, and teased hair, looking like an ad for a truck stop, wanted to slap my uppity black face.

He said, "please come into my office." I exhaled. I floated past her and flashed a Hollywood smile. I also had all the dirt on the cashier and the manager and bartender and waiters many of whom were stealing or doing something that was not kosher. Just because I wasn't in there click don't mean I didn't know where all the bodies were buried.

Well, we had a wonderful meeting. I had proof and dates and the paper trail in my expensive jacket pocket. After the meeting, he thanked me and told me to go back to my job. I got there just in time to see security lead the young cocky manager out the side door. The look he gave me was priceless. It's been said, 'God don't like ugly'.

I was the 'cockle doodle doo' at Charlie O's for a while. The entire staff had no idea how I had pulled that off, and they were all walking on eggshells around me, trying to find out if I had any dirt on them. My life is really simple. All I have ever wanted was to be left alone (I understood Garbo). I mean don't get me wrong. I like people; however, not seeing them often makes me like them even more.

After a few months the daggers continued. They knew I had been having legal troubles with my landlord about my apartment and had to go to court. I had 15 years of rent receipts in my bag that I left in the waiters changing room. One of the waiters went into my bag and stole all of my receipts the day I had to go to court. Let me repeat this in case you didn't get it. I was going to court that day, I had 15 years of rent receipts in my backpack, and someone whom I work with went into my bag and stole all of the receipts in hopes that I would lose my court case and therefore my upper east side apartment. These were my co-workers. Here's another story about the lovely little group of white' kids' I worked with.

They knew I didn't drink, and I mostly drank grape juice, so one bright sunny day someone poured wine in my grapefruit hoping I would drink it. They were a group of sick jealous vicious people. I'm a firm believer that when one lives right, and has right karma, centered, and has God in his life for real, things always work out for the best. At least in my life.

I won my court case without the rent receipts, and as an afterthought many of those nasty little people that I worked with died of strange illnesses at a very young age or had other adverse things happen in their lives . We get back what we put out.

> *"Great spirits have always encountered violent opposition from mediocre minds."*
>
> *-A. Einstein*

One of the best things about working at Charlie O's in Shubert Alley, besides the good money I made, which is the only reason I stayed as long as I did and put up with the shit I did, was the wonderful musical 'Black and Blue' starring Ruth Brown, Carry Smith and Linda Hopkins. They were three of the most talented performers on Broadway . It was in the theater across alley, and I got to meet and befriend all three ladies. They came in nightly to eat dinner and relax after the show, or sometimes before the show.

Ruth and Linda fought like cats. Friendly rivalry. It was a fabulous show. I never did get to interview Ruth, for my jazz book. We talked about it several times, and I believe her manager wanted to be paid (I can't say for sure, it's just a hunch), but my cable show is free access, and nobody got paid, not even me.) After all these years, this surely has to be a labor of love.

Ruth and I always had a hug and a warm hello whenever we saw each other. I saw her last show in New York at Au Bar, a wonderfully elegant room off Park Ave. I miss it. My kind of room. One day, I will have my own supper club and bring back the elegance I love so much.

The same thing happened with Abby Lincoln, she wanted to be on my show. We talked about it several times, but whoever was managing her at that time wanted to be paid. I don't blame them. Like the kids say, 'I ain't mad at am'. I wish I could have paid them, myself too. But I was making history.

The 1980s: The End of Drinking Was Close

After working at this restaurant for about 5 years, (the longest job I ever had) and in constant battle with these kids, one day one of the waiters got on my nerves and I slung a chair at him and wanted to take his head off. That did it. They all sighed a sigh of relief; they had finally brought me down. The union couldn't save me, not that I wanted them to, because it was God's way of saying, move on. I walked to the subway station and on the way to my apartment I said, I think I'll move to Germany.

A few weeks later, my father died, in March 1990. He was one of my best friends, a wise down- to-earth funny, and hip man, so full of life. Loved a party. Loved my mother, loved his kids, loved his work, love to dance, loved life .My father came up the hard way and made a difference. I don't think you can find one person who could say an unkind word against my father. I went home to be with my mother and family. It was the hardest thing to watch my mother. She and my father had been together 52 years. He died much too young, only 70. They were married 48 years and dated 4 years before they were wed. They were high school sweethearts.

Naturally, she went through a hard period. But she had family and friends around. Also, when Neil Bush (the President's son) and company sent the Silverado Savings and Loans into bankruptcy, which was part of the savings and loans debacle. It cut her income, and that of countless others. She was getting my father's salary from his almost 30 years at First Federal Savings and Loan, and she had to change the way she lived. She was still doing well, just not what she was used too.

I went home once or twice a year to help get the house fixed up and help with what she needed. She had family around and we all made sure she was taken care of. I, am being the youngest just wanted to do more because that's how I am. With the help of family, God and time, everything seemed to get better. My mother is my best friend and we talk almost daily from wherever I am on the planet. She went to visit a friend in Washington DC, socialite Ms. Savannah Clark; and I came back to New York.

I was unemployed again, "What's New". Oops, another song, 1939, composed by Bob Haggart, and Johnny Burke. I think I heard Sinatra's version first. Johnny Mathis' version is wonderful.

The story of my life. Out of work. Back in my New York apartment. Trying to figure out what my next move was. My phone rang. It was a young white woman who I had known for some time, on and off. She called me from Switzerland and asked me if I would accompany her to Los Angeles for her birthday. I believe she's still breathing, so it's best I call her Joan (not her real name). "Joan", I said, "I don't have money to fly to LA; but I want to wish you a great birthday and safe trip." I was about to hang the phone up when she said the trip will be my treat.

I sat up erect in bed and said, "great, detail's?". She said she would get back to me the next day. Sure enough, the phone rang, and 'Joan' said, we leave at the end of the week, and that I should meet her at the airport in Washington DC. We will be taking a private Jet to Hollywood. I cleared my throat and asked her to repeat what she has said. She did, and gave me directions to the location where the private planes leave from.

She said she may be late and I should just check in with the pilot, then get on the plane and make myself comfortable. I asked her how I would know just what plane to get on, she replied 'It will be the biggest private plane on the runway' . I still wasn't ready for all of this. But I went along with it.

She said the Airline pilot would call me to see what I wanted to be served on the flight and other details. Sure enough, he called. (That was a first for me, a pilot calling a passenger). We had a very pleasant conversation, and I told him I would like to be served a seafood dish on the flight. He told me what I would need, where to go when I arrived at the terminal, and where the private planes took off.

I make my way to Washington DC. with just enough money to buy lunch if I had to . I got there a day early and stayed overnight with my friend Tony B. Like most folks, I was used to living from paycheck to paycheck and now once again I was out of work. Also, the money I made from my night club gigs wouldn't get my clothes out of the cleaners. However, I got to the airport where the VIPs leave from and I gave security my name and ID and they took my bags and escorted me to this long and lovely and elegant plane. As the saying goes:

I'm not impressed by much, but then it doesn't take much to impress me. Well, I must say, this did It. The sight of this White sleek machine glistering in the sun. It looked so long and stately. Just sitting on the runway. Perched.

I walked in and I would have sworn I was Blake Carrington. It was replete with Marble, Chrystal, and Wealth. The hostess sat me in a leather recliner and brought me a drink of seltzer with lime. About 20 Minutes later, 'Joan 'made her entrance. A real plane Jane of an entrance. Or in this case 'plain Joan'. Stringy blond hair, no make-up, flip flops, really quite strangely dressed, but little did I know this trip would get decidedly stranger. As Margo Channing so famously said in my favorite film ever, the 1950 'Classic, *All About Eve,*' "Fasten your seat belt, it's gonna be a bumpy night." That truly is the perfect film from start to finish. It held the record of most nominated films in Hollywood history, with 14. It was tied in 1997 by *Titanic*.

We prepared to take off and after we were in flight, I found out a lot about this trip. For one, the plane we were on belonged to Michael Milking, the wealthy multi-millionaire nicknamed the "junk bond king" of Drexel, Burnham Lambert Inc., An investment banking company. In 1990, he pled guilty to securities fraud. He was sentenced to 10 years, and a 600 million dollar fine. He served 22 months in prison and has since made another fortune. He has spent the last several years helping to fight cancer.

The plane was a Gulf Stream IV. There were only a few private ones made at that time, from my understanding. Bill Cosby and Frank Sinatra (who was deeply into aviation, in fact his mom Dolly wanted him to go into Aviation. Frank Sinatra was as close to his mother Dolly as I was to my mother Cookie. He was a Sagittarius as I am, and his temper was legendary).

The Oil rich Saudi, Adnan Khashoggi, Donald Trump and Milken were some who owned Gulf Stream IV. The purpose of this trip, besides celebrating Joan's birthday, I found out fast was that she was negotiating buying this plane for several millions of dollars.

Sitting at this very large mahogany table was Joan, the man selling her this plane, and yours truly. They were in the middle of high financial dealings. I excused myself to go in the bathroom and 'slap my face and say, 'Wake Up'. I was sure I had flashbacks from the acid/LSD I had done in college, or the Heroin I had snorted years ago, or the bottles of vodka I drank, and bowls of coke I had snorted or smoked, or perhaps all of the Dolls? For surely, this wasn't real. I turned on the marble facets and splashed my face with cold water, thinking I would walk back into the room and realize I was on a Delta flight 1150 and my vivid imagination had run amok once again. But no, I had stepped into the outer limits of wealth and I soon found out, into total unmitigated folly.

The 1980s: The End of Drinking Was Close

I meet so many people in my dealings with life, I hadn't a clue where Joan and I met. But I do know that it was a while ago. I believe some woman I met while working at the 86th St. restaurant introduced us. I had no idea she was a wealthy. She drove a convertible white luxury sedan, But I'm thinking upper middle-class/ rich Westchester suburbia. I did find out that her father had a successful business in New York, and that she had married an older man who was involved in a chemical oil plant or something, and I believe she got his money after he'd died. Joan was younger than I. I was 37 at this time. She was also the inventor of a certain toy which many kids had, (and the toy will remain nameless). When it was time for dinner, I was served a rather large seafood platter on the finest of china. They each had an equally delicious lunch. We all ate, and conversation was easy. Also between "regular conversation" they discussed business about buying the plane…

After lunch, and business, the gentleman left for another part of the plane; and Joan and I sat together on a long leather sofa, alone in the room and talked side by side; sometimes holding hands, other times 'petting and cooing'. She knew my father had recently passed and she asked about my mother. I told her she was visiting her friend in Washington, DC. She said let's call her and say hello. We did; and in the middle of the conversation Joan got this bright idea, she said, "ask your mother if she wants to join us;" and without waiting on my mother's answer she instructed the pilot to turn the plan around. She took the phone and spoke with Cookie. Her concern was heartwarming.

Thank God the pilot said, we can't do that, we need landing clearance, and, this and that, and other aviation rules had to be followed, etc. . I have to admit it was a nice thought. She wanted to cheer up my mother . However, a phone call from a private plane was enough for that.

She turned to me and said, JaRon, would you have come with me on this trip had you known I was a wealthy woman? I looked her right in the eye and said, ``You will always be "just Joan" to me. That's who I met and liked from the start; this is just an extension of you. And I meant it. But slowly over the next several hours it seems like Satan entered her body and manifested itself in her soul. Once she exposed her wealth to me, she changed and became very demanding.

We landed in LA, and a car took us to our hotel. A lovely place, the name escapes me. The room they showed us, was perfectly fine for me, but not good enough for Joan; so, they showed us another room, and yet another room, and yes, another room. Finally, after several rooms 'Our Miss Joan' was content. Each room had something which displeased her. The color of the Drapes, the furniture, etc. I could have slept on the carpet. That's how tired I was. Believe it or not, I'm the most unpretentious person on earth.

We settled down for the night and fell asleep. I was mentally exhausted. Being on this private plane, in this wealthy setting was like something out of the old Hollywood movies that I love so much. I kind of expected to run into Clifton Webb or Edward G. Robinson hiding under the bed. The next day we awoke, showered together, had a lovely breakfast, then I ate her p---y so good until her toes curled.

She came like a wild goose. We both enjoyed that .Like the song says "I've got a smile on my face, for the whole human race, why It's almost like being in love," the 1947 Lerner and Loewe hit, which became a popular standard. I first heard this song many years ago on Nancy Wilson's first recording entitled "Like in Love" (1959) released in 1960. Later that evening, we wanted to watch a movie. It was one of those cable movies on the hotel room TV set. Well, it didn't come on the pay station as It was advertised, and Joan went off. She called down to the front desk and said, "I'm Ms. 'so and so', and the movie is not on and how dare you. I want someone up to my room this moment to fix it." I pretended I was busy with God knows what, as to not get involved in her madness. God knows, I had my own. When the poor man came in to fix the TV, she talked down to him in such a vile way it left a bad taste in my mouth. I let it go.

But those bouts of nastiness, and she's not even drunk, (at least I had an excuse). happened more and more. Nothing satisfied her. We would be lying in bed and she would get up at 3-4 am and call Europe and threaten lawsuits. It was a roller coaster ride. It's like she couldn't be happy, every waking moment was filled with strife and unnecessary drama. Make no mistake about it, you would be hard pressed to find anybody who loves a good drama more than yours truly, but this was just unnecessarily trite.

The next day, I called my brother Marvin to invite him out with us to dinner. We went to a nice place and nothing on the menu was to her liking, the poor waiter just stood there for what seemed an hour and I think she ended up with a slice of white bread, or something equally as appetizing. My brother and I ate like pigs and had a ball. Marvin loves to eat, drink, and have a party. But that's how we all grew up, so we come by it honestly. But dear Joan complained about everything, talked to the waiter like a piece of shit, while reeking of negative energy. She spoke to the hired help everywhere, as though they were unimportant. My brother drove us back to our hotel and I said I'd call him in a day or two. In the meantime, the way Joan spoke to the hired help was just more than I could stomach. I grew up reading Emily post and Amy Vanderbilt, and to this day 'I believe manners are a prerequisite for all that we do in life'. My Parents made me send thank you notes for everything. I still do.

Joan seemed to be devoid of that quality, but she was wealthy, and I thought she thought it gave her entitlement to be rude to people . Sad.

During this time, the comic Arsenio Hall (who was 'discovered' by Nancy Wilson and managed by her manager the great John Levy) was hot as 'catfish grease' (The Arsenio Hall Late Night TV show, and his posse. (The band consisted of Nancy Wilson's rhythm section, her ex pianist Michael Wolf, and bassist John B. Williams.

As you know by now, I had been a Nancy Wilson groupie all my life; and due to this fact, I had befriended or rather gotten to know Mike Wolf. To this day, as I mentioned earlier, I'm so grateful he played my first show when I got sober.

Mike had said, 'if you ever get to Hollywood' to call him. I got to Hollywood. I called him. Now as we all know, many people say that and when you get there the number s changed or it's unlisted and a big sign is on the door, saying 'Do Not Disturb' .This was not the case. Michael answered the phone and said he would leave my name at the gate for the taping of the show that night.

I ask Joan if she wanted to go, she said no. I said to myself, thank God. I called my brother Marvin and he was so excited, that he made plans and drove over early. Right before he got to the hotel, Joan said, I think I want to go now. I politely said, but my brother and I have made plans and he's on his way. That wasn't her concern, she wanted to go and that was that.

Now up to that point on this trip I had been a very well-behaved young man. I was praying she wouldn't have to be introduced to my other side, 'Norman Bates, 'The Protagonist in the thriller 'Psycho' - Hitchcock's 1960 masterpiece , played by Anthony Perkins. I have asked God to help me contain my temper; during my days of drugs and alcohol I would lash out and make grown folks break down into tears.

I'm sober now, but that streak is still there. When provoked. I'm working on it to this day and pray that it will get better.

The other reason for this trip, I found out was she wanted a boy toy, a pet on a leash, she wanted to put a diamond collar around my lovely chocolate neck and to be at her beck and call for sex and whatever else she wanted. And for this, she would open doors for me to stardom! What I have dreamed of all of my life. Now it was being offered to me, on a 24-carat gold platter. I believe many people in show business have had to 'perform' to get to where they are and end up hating themselves for it later down the road. (the casting couch does exist). But we do what we do and suffer the consequences later.

However, in my case, the price was too high. Nobody wanted stardom more than I. You must have realized that by now. Dear God, I ended up in a straitjacket chasing it. But this was just wrong on so many levels. I've heard that many sell their souls to Satan for stardom. Some say it's the only way to get there. I disagree. And just what is stardom? I've always wanted it, since before I knew what it is/was. More about my idea of what stardom is later.

Anyway, my dear Joan hadn't a clue as to what authentic madness was, but she was about to get just a taste. Had she met me when I had climbed into the bottle, Los Angeles would've never been the same. I explained to her that my brother was downstairs and I'm going to the taping of the show with him . She threw a fit and so did I. I don't have her money, or any money for that matter then or now, but I'll match my fits against anybody's fits.

I told her how rude and selfish and inconsiderate of people she was, and that I would never disrespect, or humiliate my brother by canceling this night he has been so looking forward to. Also, when I lose it, my voice goes up about 5 octaves, and smoke comes out of my ears. I told her that because she was wealthy didn't give her or anyone else the right to talk down to people with utter disregard, and that her parents did a poor job in raising her. She turned beet red, looked me right in my eyes and told me, 'Be very careful how you speak to me. People like me can harm you and you will never know it'. I looked at her like she had two heads, both spinning around .She was surely spewing bile from her lips. Think 'Linda Blair'. .To this day that statement gives me chills.

I left the room and went to meet my brother who was waiting downstairs, and we drove to the Arsenio Hall sound stage and Michael Wolf had wonderful seats for us. Thanks Mike. We had a ball. It was genuine energy in the room electrifying in earnest. So unlike, when years later, I went because I was invited to a taping of the Dave Letterman show and was bombarded by 20 'helpers' holding up cue cards while we were waiting in line demanding that we all scream and clap and jump up and down and show hysteria when the camera is on. How sad I thought. I told one young lady, if It's entertaining I'll show my enjoyment, but I can't fain glee for folly. This is nothing negative against the Letterman show, but It's just the way big time TV is nowadays.

Later that night I called my best friend who is my mother. Cookie, (I nor has anyone in the family or anyone who knows her ever called her anything but Cookie, as far back as we can remember) It's her nickname. We have never ever called her mom, mother, or anything maternal. I told her of my drama in Hollywood, and that I had visions of throwing Joan off the balcony. She knows me very well, she said 'sugar' leave ASAP.

Pack your things and leave . The next morning Joan was going to go shopping and I stayed by the pool sunning. One of my favorite past times, but this time I had to keep my shorts on. (The sun soothes all that is wrong in my soul.)

I was drinking virgin Pina Coladas. When she left on her shopping trip I went to the room and packed my clothes. She and I had a little game, when we were going do the nasty (have sex) we would put a rubber duck on the bed. So, I wrote a lovely note thanking her for her kind gesture of flying me to Hollywood in such luxury, and for the laughs. (What few they were,) but that it was time I went back to New York and my music. I put the note on the bed and the duck on top of the note.

I grabbed my bag and went to the lobby to get a shuttle to the airport. I used my credit card to get a ticket home. And to this day I have no idea where the money came from. But I do know that when you live right, things just seem to work out. Those things always happen for me. And I know it's God. So many people don't want to, or can't, accept blind faith. It's the only way I can walk.

> *"The reason birds can fly, and people can't is because birds have perfect faith, and to have faith is to have wings"...*
>
> *- J.M. Barrie*

I was hoping I could 'get away' before Joan of Arc returned and hopefully to avoid any scene. Wouldn't you know it; I'm walking through the lobby and in walks Joan. Our eyes met. All four of them very wide, she said are you leaving me? I said in my best "Cary Grant-ish" style, while taking her ever so gently by the elbow and escorting her toward the bar, "Joan dear, it's been a marvelous ride, but the party is over, I've overstayed my welcome, and I simply must return to New York. I left you a note upstairs thanking you for the fun. Or, as the society hostess 'Elsa Maxwell' said, "Life is a party, you joined after it started, and you leave before it is finished."

However, our Ms. Joan wanted to make an issue out of it and I was losing patience. There was no need for any further conversation. I said good-bye and walked out. She looked in shock, the fact that this struggling, Black, unemployed, broke, Jazz Musician would leave the life she was exposing me to.

Now I understand when 'Margo Channing' said, in *All About Eve* "I know I've seen better days, but I'm still not to be had for the price of a cocktail like a salty peanut." No one could say those lines like Betty Davis.

Joan waited until I was in the middle of the lobby and said rather loudly, "you can leave me now, but when you get down and out, I may take you back." Sounds like a line from a Hollywood B picture. (But then we were, after all, in Hollywood).

I flew back to Manhattan on a commercial jet but after flying on a multi-million-dollar private plane, I was not amused. I had mentioned to Joan earlier that I had a few bookings when I got back to New York. One was at a lovely Upper East Side eatery, the Sign of the Dove. A charming place. I find so few bars, clubs, restaurants inviting now-a-days; most are either sterile, devoid of warmth, or personality. Most have 20 big screen TVs each on a different channel, and loud Techno music, simply awful.

All over New York that's mostly what you find. Well not all, but the city is replete with them. I stay home. In my neighborhood, the Upper East Side, they are all side by side, for blocks and blocks. But those are the times we live in and young people love it. I've gotten old.

My goal is to open my own supper club in time and bring back the glamour of the 1940's and 50's New York. I'm sure some exist now if you are in that circle. But most of what I see today is just uninviting. Everybody in sneakers and jeans, wearing a baseball cap and holding a can of beer, while watching TV. I want a' Ricks Place' like in the 1942 classic film 'Casablanca' Starring Humphrey Bogart and Ingrid Bergman, Claude Rains. Paul Henreid etc.

I had worked the Sign of The Dove before. While I was in Hollywood I was re- booked. This time with Frank Gant on drums, Lloyd Myers on Piano (he had played for Sammy Davis Jr.) and great Bassist Earl May (who was at one time married to singer Gloria Lynn).

The famous gossip columnist, then and now, Cindy Adams lived at that time, a few blocks from me on east 86th St. and Fifth Ave. I would leave fliers of my upcoming shows with her doorman, hoping she would one day catch my show.

It was a Saturday night and the place was always packed. My family was of course there, as they are always for important events in my life. That's what families are for. I'm pacing the floor because the band is nowhere to be found. We were to hit at 9pm. by 10.30 it was clear that the band was not going to show up. I was overcome with disappointment. It had the promise of a wonderful night; and sitting in the room was Cindy Adams. I left the club after trying to explain to the manager of Sign of the Dove why my band didn't show up. It was the first time it has ever happened in my life. I was devastated.

I wanted a drink of vodka;, no I wanted a bottle of vodka. and a bowl of cocaine. But, I let go and let God.

The next day I sat up erect in bed and I remembered the words Joan said to me in the midst of our argument. "Be very careful how you speak to me, people like me can harm you and you will never know it."

I put it out of my mind as the rantings of a mad jealous rich woman. who didn't get what she wanted. Namely me. A few weeks later I had a booking at a club called Marty's. Not the famous one on 73rd and third Avenue, where Nancy Wilson, Joe Williams, Mel Torme, Carmen McRae and other headliners played but they had another place in the east 50s, on 55th street off third Avenue. I had done lots of advertising for this show I had a wonderful rhythm section and was raring to go. The night before my show, I got on my bicycle and rode to the club to do any last-minute things which needed to be done. It was the night before I was there, and it was in full swing. (You see I have always been my agent, publicist, manager, gofer, etc.). that hasn't changed. And I'm tired. But we do what we have to do to get to where we are going. I wish I had someone to do these things for me, but I don't. So, we do what we have to do, I don't believe in waiting on anyone to do anything for me . Just get out of my way and I'll do it for myself. When I got to Marty's, there was a big sign on the door, saying club closed until future notice, with a big pad chain lock on the door. One night before my opening, . I thought of Joan.

"Be very careful how you speak to me, People like me can harm you and you will never know it." By the way, the club was open the very next day after my gig was supposed to have happen. Ummm…That next month I had a booking at a wonderful club in the village called Carlos off 6th avenue. My gig was canceled without any explanation. When I called the club was I was rudely told I had no gig there. Again I thought of Joan. 'Be careful how you talk to people like me, I can harm you and you will never know it"

I said then and I say now, had I been able to prove it 100% that she was behind this I would've lashed out and I can't imagine what I might have done, I dare not think of it. I will let nothing or no one get in the way of my career. My dear friend Norbert has told me for years, not to worry about people who behave like that. He says they are already punished by being who they are.

I met a guy who became one of my best friends in life Norbert Bogner. I bike daily in New York's Central Park, and all over New York. We both got bikes at Larry's Bike Shop on East 85th St. near my home... My dear friend Jeanette married Larry. One day, while biking in the park, I ran into Norbert. He was on his bike which he also. This was late 1989. He was living with his wife at that time. I found out later, they were in the process of splitting up and he was looking for a place to stay. He had come to New York from Austria and was still learning English and the American way. He had a wonderful job with a famous Diet Doctor for the A list. - Stephen Gullo.

Remember when I threw a chair at my co-worker at Charlie O's and said I was moving to Berlin? I told Norbert of my plans to go to Berlin Germany, and when that happens, perhaps he could keep/house, sit my apartment. Since I knew no one in Berlin and didn't speak the language, and Norbert did, that was a tremendous help. And after the last few club dates I had which were mysteriously canceled, I felt it best I leave town before I do something I'd regret.

I had a few dollars from one of my last jobs, at least enough to get my ticket and a cheap place for a while, and with Norbert keeping the apartment for me and paying the rent, I had extra money to really delve into Berlin and my music. Norbert got on the phone and helped me find a Pension in Berlin (a small cheap Hotel) he booked it for me in his native language, German. Actually, his language is Austrian, very close. I packed my bags, gave him my house keys and said the apartment was yours, look after it until I get back. Just like that.

Right before I left a friend who worked at NBC called me and said JaRon I understand you are moving to Berlin, I have a friend there who speaks English and he can help you get to the Hotel and maybe show you around. Here is his number.

I decided to move to a different land, from the time when I threw the chair at the waiter while working as a waiter at Charley O's. First I went home to help my mother after my father's death, and then going on this space Odyssey to Hollywood with the wealthy woman who wanted a boy toy. About two- three months had passed. I packed everything I thought I needed and left on my journey. People thought I had lost my mind. But others who really know me, know that when I say something, I will make it come true. 'If It's the last thing I do'. Do you hear a song? Come on, It's your turn. Great song.

However, this time. I was a basket case. This wasn't like taking a vacation for a week, I was planning to move to Berlin Germany to work on my music and get a fresh start career-wise, come home every few months to check on my apartment, etc. Anyway, that was the plan. On the plane I was sweating bullets. Scared, yet very excited, not knowing anyone in this strange land of millions of people who didn't look like me, not speaking their language, not knowing if I would like them or if they would like me. It was a major move. But it didn't matter, it was the choice I made, I'm sure it came from my higher power, from that inner force which guides me, which guides us all if we allow ourselves to tap into it. Don't block the blessings. Be open to receive them.

But, what was I thinking when I decided after throwing a chair at a co- worker, riding home on the subway that I should move to Berlin?

Of all the countries worldwide, of all the Gin Joints in all the towns, I could have decided to go anywhere. It was the change I needed, and I was sure the place for me was Berlin, Germany. I had never been there. Go figure. God was speaking, and I heard him. When one is seeking answers, we must be still to hear them.

"The Law of Success"

> *When the consciousness is kept on God, you will have no fears; every obstacle will then be overcome by courage and faith, "A wish is desire without energy. After a wish may come "Intention," the plan to do a thing, to fulfill a wish or desire. But 'will' means I act until I get my wish. When you exercise your willpower you release the power of life's energy, not when you merely wish passively to be able to obtain an objective."*
>
> *-Paramahansa Yogananda*

There I was, flying to Berlin, Germany . So many things were going on in my head. But I never lost focus. I called the number my friend from NBC had given me from before I left New York. The person I called was named Karl Gunterman. He was a very tall man with a beard, who wore glasses on his nose and usually looked over them.

He looked about 60 years old. I had called him before I left New York to tell him I was coming to Berlin, and to say hello . He said he would meet me at the airport, but I said, "please don't bother, I'll take a taxi to the Hotel and call you when I got settled." THANK GOD, Karl came to the airport to meet me. When I arrived in Berlin, it was in the midst of the reunification of East/West Germany November1989 and it was millions of people in town. The Berlin Wall had come down and it was a joyous, festive time. With all of the Germans coming together, it was something to see.

Karl and I went to my Hotel that Norbert had booked for me, but they looked at me like I had just escaped from the nut house. Growling at me, in German. (the German language sounds very hard) and I was clueless as to what they were saying; but I gathered they had no time for a young Black American and dismissed me. They had given my room away. It was like New Year's Eve, so every Hotel was full.

We went to another Hotel, and yet another Hotel and after several Hotels, Karl turned to me and said," JaRon I have a large 2-bedroom apartment in the center of town, why don't you stay with me tonight; and tomorrow, we will get you a hotel. Never had I heard kinder words. I had been up 36 hours, too nervous to sleep before I left, and was just worn out. We got back to his apartment, and his address was the equivalent to living on East 86th St. near 5th Ave., Close to where I live in NYC. He lived right off the Kurfuerstendamm at Adenauer-Platz.

I had no idea Karl was, shall we say 'eccentric', until he opened the door to his apt in this lovely building. There were old newspapers, and other 'stuff' stacked up from floor to ceiling in all 6 rooms of this very large expensive apartment. I had to turn sideways to enter the apartment. He showed me to my room, and I could not find the bed, I swear I could not find it. He threw some stuff to the floor and there was this huge bed. As tired as I was, it looked like the Taj Mahal. I was deeply grateful. You have no idea. I couldn't began to describe how tired I was. Comatose comes close. I thanked him and crawled into a bed that had not been cleaned since 1869 and I slept for 16 hours.

I woke up and met Karl in earnest. We had tea and talked for hours. I was so tired last night that I hadn't noticed that Karl was as cripple as he was. He lived on the 3rd floor of a 5th for walk up. He walked with a cane. The kitchen, and I kid you not, hadn't seen soap and water in several years. I will try and explain this abode, hold on. 'Tight'. As the singer Betty Carter (1929- 1998) sang" on her album called *Finest Hour*. She was without a doubt one of the greatest 'Pure Jazz' Vocalists in history.

It was a lovely apartment with high ceilings, (leave it to me to leave Manhattan and end up on the most famous street in Germany) but the dirt and junk was overwhelming. You had to walk sideways to get in and out of every room. There was newspapers and muck piled up from floor to ceiling in every room of the apartment. The kitchen table had enough space for one plate to fit, while he ate. When I arrived, he moved something and made space for my plate or cup, you couldn't have both at a time, so I put the cup on the floor and plate on the table when I ate. It was absolutely disgusting. I wish I had pictures to share with you. But I don't .I think I was one of the few people who ever entered the apartment. Norbert came to visit once and he's still in shock. He collected stuff. It's like someone Removed the ceiling and a garbage truck emptied a ton of trash in the apartment. I kid you not.

The floors had not been swept, let along mopped, since he moved in years earlier. The fridge had never been cleaned EVER. Nor the inside of the windows. (the building workers cleaned the out sides). God forbid if I moved something or tried to clean. The bathroom tub had changed colors, and each room of this wonderful large apartment was full, from floor to ceiling. I found out later, he wanted it like that. So that was the name of that tune. While in Rome do what the Romans do. I later found out by watching Oprah the names for this disease are Hoarde and clutter syndrome, Tunnel living, or Obsessive-compulsive disorder. OCD. He was a severe hoarder of the highest order.

We got to know each other over tea, and he proposed to me that I could pay him to rent the room for a few weeks until I got my bearings. It was perfect. I could pay cheap rent and help him by shopping, and doing a few errands, since he was a cripple. It worked out perfect for us both. He had a way of looking over his glasses while speaking to me as though I were a complete idiot. He was very German. So, I played the role. I was in the center of town, and that's all I needed to let Germany know that I was here.

Also, Karl afforded me that opportunity. The first few days I spent walking all over Berlin getting lost, just sightseeing, not knowing anyone, or anything about the city. Each night I came back to the apartment, Karl would stare at me. It seems like he was shocked I was smart enough to make it back home. Sometimes I think he had not seen many Black people before. But I had a bed to call mine, and that was all that mattered. I was sure it was temporary. This went on for a few weeks. I would try and cook dinner for us both (I like to think I'm good cook if you like Louisiana foods. As I mentioned earlier my goal is to open up my own jazz cafe in time).

But in that kitchen, it was not possible. So, he ate local German food out of containers, and I made do .It seemed as long as I was the needy Black guy from America I was very welcomed in his home. The little lost American, living a fantasy of being a jazz singer and performing in Berlin. A fool full of fantasy/ dream's or so he thought. *Who can refute a sneer?*

But me being, well me, stumbled upon a private chic club in the center of town, called Chez Alex' The rumor was that it was run by 'Russian business types' or mob. Berlin has a large Russian population.

Anyway, it was the kind of club where you had to knock on the door, and someone would open and peak through this square in the door and if they liked you, you got in. Kind of like studio 54 and the red velvet ropes places. I never liked places like that, then or now; and I don't go, period. Ever. People who stand in line and let some idiot judge whether or not you meet the criteria to gain admittance are, dare I say, fools? Shame on me, maybe that's too harsh of a word. I'll try and think of another one; but think about it, you stand there and some person who spends more money on chewing gum then books looks at you or over you and says, 'this one or that one can come in, but not this one or that one'. I mean, *please. How silly. What low self-esteem.* But, people put themselves in that position to be judged . Go figure.

It reminds me of the reality TV shows today where people judge the talent of others. It's strictly their opinion, nothing more or nothing less. Some people love Billie Holiday. Some people hate Billie Holiday. So, if Lady Day is singing on one of these shows In front of the judge who hates her, she's off the show. Simply because of his opinion.

Yet they have been given power to decide your future. Maybe I'm just crazy, but I could never allow myself to be subjected to that. Also, I'm sure, that the singers I have learned from, these people judging these shows have no idea who they are, so how can they judge me? Today, unless you sound like everybody else singing through the nose and following a formula of today's culture, it wouldn't work for me.

I had passed this club a few times and 'hid' across the street and watched how it worked. Only the pretty people got in, in fancy cars, fancy dressed, upper-crust types. In other words: Players, Pimps,

Hookers, and Whores. Like how I grew up in Louisiana and how I lived in New York. It was a breeze.

I got dressed one night and made my way to Chez Alex. I knocked on the door, and I was invited in. It was what I expected, pretty people, loud music, loud showy conversations, drinks flowing, and a big piano to the side, not being used that night. I had a drink and being the only Black person in the club that night and looking like a movie star the owner came over and wanted to know who I was. I told him, we talked, laughed, swapped stories and he played the piano and I sang a song. Before I left the club 45 minutes later, I had a booking every Sunday night for a month.

It was not much money (100 dollars) per man, per show, It's the same now in New York, in most clubs, if that; most people work for the door, nowadays . Club owners are cheap in New York, and the talent in most of the clubs reflects it. You get what you pay for. Many club owners want the artist to pack the house every night, every show, do all the advertising, and for so little money. I think the owners should bring in their own crowd It's your club, and my job is to entertain them and keep them there and coming back. Most of the talented musicians are struggling, unless you are a marquee name. But this is the business we chose, so deal with it.

My dear friend Alma Carroll in Brooklyn wife of Be-Bop singer Joe Carroll said when the club owners would complain to him about the turn out for his show, he would say, listen. 'You get the people in here; I'll get them to spend money'.

I had landed a steppingstone to the next tier and realized that my friends were more important than the money I was going to be paid. I could use this club to get my name around Berlin. Alex was a very popular club, which I had no idea. I was only in town a few weeks.

So, when I came back very excited to the apartment and told Karl my good news, I was met with stony silence, and finally a "how did you manage that so fast?" If I had a dollar for every time someone has said that to me. I'd have enough money for my nightclub by now. (Which reminds me, 15 years later I was told the same thing by the Owner of a Japanese club where I worked for a few years on tour.) I went to do 13 weeks at his club; but managed to perform at the world's fair which was being held in Nagoya, Japan in 2005. When the club owner saw my picture in the largest paper in Japan, he snapped,' how did you manage this so fast'? You move too fast. I don't understand why I have to wait until someone else decides when I can do whatever it is that I'm doing. Life is too short to just wait. I won't let life pass me by. I will take every opportunity that God brings my way. Period. So, get over it. I have always lived by my rule "I will define myself and work diligently to make it a reality."

But in Japan, It's a cultural issue. So, it's a little different. However, I'm very grateful for the opportunity he gave me to perform in his wonderful Japanese club. *Back to Berlin and Karl.*

I found that statement strange coming from Karl. I didn't entertain it. (but I keep a mental record of everything in the reservoirs of my mind). He asked me questions about did I know what kind of place it was? And the kind of showy people who went there, etc. All negative comments. He made references to the Russian Mafia who frequented the place. I said it's no different from most nice clubs in New York or Paris, or Tokyo, or any other place.

My concern was, it was a lovely room with a grand piano and a good sound system, in which I could be heard and 'Start spreading the news'. *Oops another song, Your turn.*

Tainted

I Found out, there was another Black performer who worked there. An American. A great guy named Rashiddi. He has lived there for a while and he was happy there. He was married to a nice German girl and they had a daughter. Today many years later, he has his own cafe in Berlin, which I visited.. I'm so happy for him, he stayed there and made it work. I love that. It's so easy to just give up. Half the battle is just showing up. In fact, my very first gig in Berlin I worked with Rashiddi on piano, and it was fun. When I was in Berlin last year he was at my show at the Badischer Hof., a hip jazz club.

My opening night was a success, except for one thing. I wanted a new look when I moved to Berlin, so I shaved the hair on my head before I left New York for a bald/shaved look. I ran out of razors that I had brought, and the night of my opening I used a razor I bought in Berlin. I wasn't used to it and cut myself in the head while shaving. A few hours before show time. I was a wreck. I had to perform wearing a beret the entire night. Not one of my finest on-stage dress statements.

The word got out around town. Soon every Black American musician knew I was there and in time I worked with all of them in some compactly or another. One of the best Pianists anywhere is Reggie Moore, and it was a joy to work with him and the bassist Earl Bostic. I remember Reggie from many years earlier when he worked at Trudy Heller in New York's Greenwich Village. I just found a video with me and Reggie from that period and told his lovely wife Cornilia just this week, 2019.

I met many fine German musician Thomas Fassnau on Bass and Sherry Bertram on drums and so many others. I probably worked with every one of the good musicians while I was living there and when I came back there on tours there over the years.

But when you are the new kid on the block and move too fast without 'their permission', it ruffles feathers. And the green-eyed monster began to rare it's ugly and ever-present head. And I'm still ruffling feathers. I just don't know how to 'stay in my place', won't sit back and wait for the powers that be to let me know when it's OK. When you can take a step forward. *Simon Says?*

Chez Alex was my introduction to the nightclub scene in Germany. All was going along according to my wishes and thoughts. God's will. Also, I had enrolled in the Goethe institute, the best school to learn German, so I was told. I met a wonderful guy who was in my class, Gary Harrison, from the west coast in America. We talked last week also, and it's 2019. He showed friends, Iris and Jo, who were visiting Berlin for the first time, a great time just last month.. He speaks perfect German and has lived there since we met in 1990.

One day I was late, as usual, and leaving Karl's apartment running down the stairs going to class and coming up the stairs was a young lady. When we passed each other, she said hello and I said hello, and we started laughing uncontrollably. It was the funniest thing. I will never forget it. I said, "I'm late for class," and I gave her a flier to come see me at Alex.

She lived upstairs from Karl. I had never seen her before. But she had seen me entering and exiting the apartment building. Anyway, she came to see me that next week and she could not get in. She's not the fancy type. She's a school teacher in one of Berlin's better schools with understated elegance and class, as opposed to the high glamour of the showy Chez Alex set.

We ran into each other a few days later, and she mentioned she came to see me and couldn't get in, but she was coming back this week. She came back and this time got in and enjoyed the show. We had drinks afterwards. (I only drank juice). And we talked and talked and talked. I think I did about 5 or 6 shows at this club. Then other acts came in.

I told her the man I was living with was completely mad. She had an idea because once she had to go into his apartment because he had fallen down or something and she never recovered either from what she had seen. I think she still has nightmares. Poor thing. But nobody ever went to visit, so it was not common knowledge.

Living with Karl had gotten so bad that I truly believe he was trying to kill me. Well, that may be an over-statement, But He grew to hate me because I was living my life in Berlin. Hate is such a strong word, but his feelings for me were very strange and I wasn't sure why except that I was doing what I wanted to do. But then, I always have.

I don't know any other way. You should try it. Like *Auntie Mame* the 1958 classically funny film starring the great actress Rosalind Russell. The Patrick Dennis Novel was a major success. Mame throws her hands up in the air and proclaims, 'Live! Life's a Banquet and most poor suckers are starving to death'. Live……… I do, Mame. I live.

I also kept my end of the deal by going shopping for Karl, doing other errands and being there to help him. He couldn't understand how this Black American could come here by himself and do all the things that I was doing. After a while, He tried to sabotage me. He would leave booby traps in the apartment. For instance, when I would come home at 4 am, he would have the telephone cord pulled very tight across the hallway from my room to his room about 2 inches from the floor, in pitch darkness, so I would get my foot caught in it and tumble to the floor.

When I'd open the door, the reflection from the hall lit up the entrance, so I could see the trap he had set. I wouldn't acknowledge it and stepped carefully over it. But wouldn't you know it, the poor fool would wake up and forget he had set a trap for me and fall down every time. I thought it was the funniest thing. I would put a sock in my mouth in my room and scream with laughter. I would go out to help him up and say, 'oh my God Karl, what happened?' Once he looked into my eyes over his glasses sprawled out on the floor and said, "you are just so damn clever."

I'd play dumb, like I hadn't a clue as to what he was talking about then feign interest in his well-being. He would do many things like that. He would leave a cup right at the edge of the cluttered table where if you just pass by the wind would knock it down. He wanted and prayed for me to knock it down so he could have something to get on me about, something to say, see? But every time it was poor Karl who would knock it down and I'd pick it up and say 'Karl are you OK, my dear friend? After several weeks turned into months of this, we were both going mad. Remember, when one sets a trap for someone, you better set two, 'cause you will surely get caught in it.

He wanted me gone and I wanted to go. I had made friends in Berlin and was performing and having a ball We were getting to the point where one of us might attack the other. The lady I met on the stairwell, Margrit, has been one of my nearest and dearest friends since we met. (We talked yesterday and it's August 2019) She told me the next day that she and her boyfriend Manfred were going to Greece for six weeks, and would I keep their apartment. All we have to do is let go and let God. For real, and things fall into place. Every time.

It was a true blessing, Margrit had a fabulous apartment. Huge rooms, high ceiling, Terrace, baby grand piano, hard wood floors, 2 bedrooms, very large living room and den, It's a lovely home, huge bathroom and huge tub. Lovely kitchen, which I loved to cook in.

They left me the keys and off they went. I had my own place for 6 weeks in the heart of town. I would check in on Karl from time to time, but he was becoming more and more angry and aloof. I was and will always be deeply grateful to him for giving me my start in Berlin. Without him, my time there would have much different and I'm sure, not nearly as nice. I do deeply believe that everything happens for a reason.

Of the millions of people in Berlin, why did I end up with Karl? He was so strange and had become so mean, and erratic in behavior. I found out years later that he had a severe brain tumor, and it was slowly killing him and causing bizarre behavior. Nobody knew it. They finally had to put him away. He is forever in my prayers. Thank you Karl for your help when it was truly needed.

Living in Margrit's large elegant apartment off the Kurfurstendamm was like living in a Hollywood movie. Well, where else would you expect me to live? But then, most of my life has been a movie of sorts as far as I'm concerned. I was meeting all the right people in the music business, and one was a big (in size and fame) blues. gospel singer by the name of Queen Yanah, and her manager PJ, January Watts. We all became best friends, Queen was famous in Berlin, and is still performing. It was so good to have Black Americans living in Berlin, where I could go, visit, and I did often. I would ride my bike to their apartment 3-4 am after Queens night club shows. We would watch movies and laugh and eat late into the day.

Sometimes I'd fall asleep right on the floor watching movies, it was wonderful. PJ died in 1996 and she is missed. A wonderfully funny lady. She got to hear my second CD, "Sounds Good To Me", and loved it.

When Margrit and Manfred returned I had to find another home. (Because I have traveled to so many countries and lived on so many people's sofas, to this day I take in people from all over the world and I always will. It's stressful to be in a strange country with little money and staying in a Hotel will eat up all the money. Everywhere I went, or I go to this day, there's a sofa where I can sleep, so when they come to New York, my home is theirs.

My first big pay day New Year's Eve show @ Hotel Sylter Hof, Berlin 1990 – Margrit, Me, & Cookie, My mother

In my travels through Berlin I met someone who was also going on holiday and they gave me their keys for 6 weeks, and this went on for a long while, until I met a German girl named Adeline. She was a sweet girl and I loved the way she smelled. I love a women to smell like a woman ... the scent of a women is what the attraction is or should be between people. I don't want perfumes in my bed, and neither did she, we enjoyed each other a great deal. I want to smell her, taste her. Not Channel #5.

Comic Legend, George Carlin, who I adored has a great routine about dogs. Just watch Dogs. They have the right idea. Well people are also animals; but today, especially Americans. Everybody sprays 10 different kinds of perfume and cologne, and deodorants and powders, and Oils, it's enough to make me vomit.

Any who, I moved in with her for a short while. We had a good time. But, I don't like anyone asking me where I'm going and when I'm coming and what time can they expect me. That's why I live alone to this day. I'm very jealous of my privacy. I can't take 20 questions. It drives me nuts. Too clingy. Having a woman around the house all day is like having a piano in the kitchen. It's beautiful, and nice to look at, but after a while it just gets in the way. Whenever I do get in a serious relationship, we must have a large home with separate rooms. Maybe live across the street from one another. Or in a different city?

That relationship was short lived. We had great sex and fun, but please don't cling to me. I've been in a straitjacket once.

I eventually found my own apt, and because Norbert was helping by keeping my apartment in New York, and that helped support what I was doing. Never have I had such a friend to offer financial support so completely. A true blessing. (but then, you will read, and have read in this book, I'm blessed). I always have been.

The 1980s: The End of Drinking Was Close

Me and Amy Quint

Margrit became my manager, and I worked on and off in Berlin for 2 years. She did this for no money, (not that I was making much anyway) but, simply because she's special and wanted to help a friend. She is a magnificent woman. She got me my first $2,500.00 gig. I made some wonderful friends there which I still have to this day. As I said earlier, when I make friends, It's usually for life. Thank you Margrit.

I moved back to New York after 2 years, then went back to Berlin for the next 4-5 years on tour to work a few small jazz clubs. After working on and off in clubs and living life doing what we do, I came back to NYC and got a local Jazz TV show in 1994, which I still have today; where I interviewed many of the Jazz greats from Nancy Wilson and Oscar Peterson, Joe Williams, Clark Terry, Dr. Billy Taylor, Anita O'Day , George Carlin, Sonny Fortune, and so many more. I was archiving these legends. You can read their stories in my book, *Historical Jazz Conversations.* I needed money and fast, I was introduced to a way to make money without leaving my home.

With all of my talent, and nowhere to let it out, I'd go mad if I didn't have an "open" mind. I looked around at all that passes for talent today, and I'm relegated to writing sex stories for web sites to pay rent. Sinatra wouldn't make it in today's musical climate.

I had to let out my demons and rage and I did it through writing fetish bizarre sex tales, a form of therapy and it worked. And if you don't have demons, then you are taking up air. and if you don't have a fetish, then you are basically in everybody's way. Everybody's got some shit/baggage. Some more than others.

I think it kept me sane, I could visit Satan and dance with the devil, and click my heels and back to reality. But is it 'Live or is it Memorex. (if you're over 60 you will get this reference). Think Ella.

I believe anyone who can't let go 100% in their sexual fetishes, in the dark places of the mind while masturbating, then they should not be allowed to masturbate. And if your toes don't curl at the climax, then, you ain't doing it right, and you should just retire, get a gold watch and sit and watch the *Golden Girls*, or *Leave it to Beaver*.

But once our mental sexual peccadillos are judged as moral or immoral, then it's all over folks. The mind is sacred. and a terrible thing to waste, as NAACP can tell you and has told us for 50 years.

Like Tina Turner, I don't do anything nice and easy, I do it nice and rough. So, I delved into deeply perverted sex fantasies and was able to pay my rent without leaving my home and that gave me the time and energy to work on my book, and music, and TV show, and documentary, etc. I have never been able to work 9-5. Ever. I just can't, it's not in my DNA. Never have been and never will be. I accepted it when I was 16. And besides, I had too many important things I had to do to waste time making money 9-5.

Unless you think like everybody, and look like everybody, dress like everybody, or sound like everybody, act like everybody; then something is very wrong with you. And in today's political climate, big brother is more real than even George Orwell envisioned. But we must remember a perverted sexual fetish is in one's mind, not in one's soul . It's what we do, not what we say that really matters.

However, being a libertine myself, I believe one's sexual thoughts should soar to the outer limits. I've always said, there's two places one can have no inhibitions, on stage, and in sex. On stage one has to strip naked to get the core of one's performance.

Once restrictions are placed on our thoughts we are dead. but I shall never bow to conformity.

Chapter 5

The Nightmare Starts

One day in 2009 around 6.30 AM. I got a knock on my apartment door. I opened the door and in rushed maybe 10 white policemen hands on guns, encircling me. They push me to a chair and, ask, 'Do you have any guns or drugs in the apartment?" I, who have never been in trouble in my life ever, said, "Of course not, unless you planted them in my home". The policeman looked into my eyes and said, "if I were you, I'd take this very seriously." All of the life poured out of me at that moment.

I had no idea what this could be about, and when I found out the charge, it was so shocking and unbelievable that to this day I shudder to remember it. A case so vile and disturbing most people never recover. I did. Here is my story. A story which has to be told to save others from this madness and let the world know that things aren't always what they seem to be. People are being destroyed nationwide and many permanently, due to overzealous prosecutors, antiquated laws, racist untruthful police officers, corrupt lawyers and a justice system replete with folly. Putting people in prison is American Big Business! Some of us, I believe, have to go for a purpose not known until much later. I was one of them.

I had just returned to New York from a trip to Baton Rouge Louisiana, by way of Berlin Germany to take my dear and wonderful mother out of a nursing home and put her back into her large and comfortable home, where she and I felt she belonged. My mother and I had a very special relationship, as I did with my father who died in 1990, much too early. In 2008 my mother 'Cookie', 85 years old, suffered a stroke and my family, like most families today thought a nursing home was the best solution.

Maybe it was because I was the youngest child, spoiled, talked to my mother daily since I moved to New York in 1972, We would have battles, all-out war, curse each other out often, then have a big laugh and have a big dinner. She is still my best opponent in a good fight, but you better not do anything to her, because you would have to deal with me.

As I said earlier in this book Cookie came to visit me in Europe, and she was at my first big show in Berlin that Margrit booked me for - New Year's Eve in 1990. We had one of our famous fights sooner or later, and I had to put her out of my apartment and two friends of mine, Yahna and her manager PJ - January Watts was delighted to have my mom stay there for a few days. I called daily to check on her. After a few days, she was back. We left Berlin and went to Paris where we had a grand time, and major fights on the Champs Elysees. We were in the middle of a hot and heated discussion when she turned to me and said, I'll scratch your face. Then she looked at me and I looked at her; and we just screamed with laughter, because I said, that would be the last thing you do. We laughed so hard we had to sit on a bench to catch our breath. Then we ducked into a lovely quaint bistro and had brunch.

The issue was we were just alike. My father spoiled my mother, as he should have done; and they both spoiled me. They were both beautiful people with movie star looks, and sometimes volatile tempers. Deeply in love for over 50 years, Think Liz and Dick. So, I come by whatever I am naturally.

No matter how hard my mother and I fought, we were best friends and had a deep unshakable bond that few could understand. Once in the late 1960s my mother and I were leaving a store and walking to her brand-new bronze Fleetwood Cadillac when a man she knew came to the car and she put the window down. They were talking and laughing and after a while they said bye. She put up the window and we drove off,.. then she shook her head still laughing and said, 'um um um; that Robert is as happy as a sissy with a dick in his mouth'.

I kid you not. I was stunned! We both laughed as we did about so many things in life. This was long before PC speak. But I shouldn't have been shocked, because she was an earthy woman, kinda like a Margo Channing character.

Once, years later when my mother was visiting me and my sister's family in New Jersey for Christmas, which was a tradition after my father passed, my niece (who like her mother is simply beautiful and a real lady) was in college and sitting at the dinner table saying that she needed money for this, and for books, and for that, rent, and she needed a job, etc.. my mother in all her 'fabulousness' while sipping gin, said with a straight face "Baby you are sitting on your money maker." Of course, my dear sister almost passed out and my niece went into a state of shock.

I, on the other hand, applauded it and found it would have made a great line in a Billy Wilder film. So that's just a part of our relationship. Remember we talked daily since I moved to New York. I was never a mama's boy, don't get it twisted.... we just rolled like that. And I'm grateful for these memories; and one reason for this book is to release a lot of pent up anger and rage for being put in prison for a Lie, and to remember my wonderful dear friend, Cookie.(The first thing she said upon hearing I was in jail was, "It's a lie, someone set you up".)

The Nightmare Starts

When I called my brother Marvin and was told that Cookie was in a nursing home, I said, "I thought it was premature (remember I was in Berlin) and let's wait awhile. These things can turn around and I said, "God hasn't spoken yet, so, I want to wait to hear what God has to say on this."

But, they all felt it was best. because she could not speak and it was a massive stroke, everybody has to grapple with this family situation in their own way. It's an American dilemma. We just saw it differently. I called Cookie in the hospital and her speech had started to come back, I asked her how she was feeling and was she comfortable where she was, and what did she want to do? She said she wanted to go home, So, I said, "Then, I'll come and take you home, stay there and get your strength, do your therapy, or whatever you have to do, and I'll be home in a week to get you. She said, "You promise??" I said, "count on it."

Now, remember, I'm now as I was then, a struggling jazz artist/entertainer, with little to no funds, and in Berlin Germany in 2009. I had only been there 36 hours before talking to my brother and getting this news about Cookie. I was in Berlin to pick up a few small gigs and enjoy doing what it is I do. I had to get home to help my mother, so I started calling airlines to get a cheap flight home to New York. Everyone said it would cost me several hundred dollars to get a ticket back to New York or to change my travel date, I explained that I had just gotten to Berlin a day ago, and now my mother is sick and needs me back home. I have little money to get a ticket and need help. Not one airline would assist me to get home unless I could pay several hundred dollars I didn't have. I was staying with a dear friend, Henry Block, in Neukoelln .

So I went to bed and prayed, hard. I woke up the next day and got back on the phones trying to get home to my mother. I spoke with a lady on the phone and told her my story of having to get back to New York, I don't remember the airline now, but this wonderful soul said to me, "I hear you, and I'll get you home." And for $25.00, this saint got me on the plane heading home.

That's the universal God.

Arriving back in New York, I got to my apartment and packed a few things and hopped in my Lil Toyota Tercel driving to Baton Rouge. A very long drive, indeed. I will spare you all the gory details; but as I promised my mother I took her out of the nursing home and stayed with her for several weeks and got aids and all the other help; and she lived at home for a while in her surroundings and was happy. While she was in the nursing home the Eames family home was being put up for sale, but when my mother came home, that didn't happen. And as you will see shortly in the book, it saved my life.

After just a few days, my mother was in the kitchen making me my favorite dishes, after being in a nursing home a few days earlier. Amazing. The power of God.

After several weeks Cookie was back to her fighting weight, and we were at it in full battle mode. I had to buy brand new boxing gloves. We went into our corners of the ring, and we cussed each other out, one of our most famous fights. Think Ali-Frazer, the thrilla in Manila. It was simply magnificent. I laughed all the way home, I knew she was back.

Well, I knew my duty here was done and I made plans to leave Baton Rouge, heading home to New York.

You see when that knock came to my door and the police rushed in.

The Nightmare Starts

You see when that knock came to my door the first time, I'd only been back in NYC 48 hours after driving back from Baton Rouge Louisiana, taking care of my mother. I opened the door and a white gentlemen standing identified himself as a police officer, saying there had been a robbery in the neighborhood and wanted to know if I had seen anything since my apartment faces East 85th St. I said no. He asked if I lived alone. I said I do. He said, have a good day, and left. My white laptop, sitting right on the small table next to the door where the officer and I had been chatting, in plain view, and I believe he even asked if that was my laptop I said it was., I didn't think about it at all, of course, until hindsight, after I was arrested and jailed and piecing all the parts together.

I'm a very spiritual person and I have a profound relationship with God. I always have since before I came through my mother's birth canal, it's a oneness, which guides and protects me.

I'm blessed and highly favored as black folks say in the church.(I am not a church going person, it's just not for me) But I never knew how much until God forced me to surrender while in prison.

I dropped this same white computer, which the police saw, while I was in Baton Rouge and broke it. I had taken it to the Apple store on East 23rd St. in NYC the day I got back to have it repaired; but it was too expensive, so I decided to just try and save my music, and tv archives on the computer.

I'm lying in bed, sleeping around 4 am and I heard a voice say to me.' throw that computer away now'. I did not miss a beat, I jumped out of bed, never questioning what was said to me, or by whom, or for what reason, but I listened. It was early July 2009. So, I put on shorts, t-shirt, sneakers, and grabbed that white Apple laptop sitting on the small table by the door that the police officer saw, and ran 4 blocks to the east river, and the voice said, throw it away. I did. Right into the East River.

Less than 48 hours later is when I heard the second knock on my door, and it was life-altering. Unless you have been through an event like this, it's unimaginable.

When the police rushed in and surrounded me my world changed forever, as would yours. In rushed maybe a dozen white cops with hands-on holstered guns. They said to me where is the stash? I asked, "stash of what? They said, "child porn." I said you are in the wrong place.

Then they showed me a still photo they said came from a video that displayed a white man and a white woman having sex with a little girl and the little girl had her hand in the woman's vagina. and that I made the video. I was in complete and unequivocal shock. To this day I cannot get it out of my mind. Later, in a report it was written by one of the officers or someone involved with this case, that said that I was the mastermind behind an international child porn ring and devil worshiper who killed, drank the blood and sacrificed children.

As I write this today, almost 10 years later, tears flow.

While looking at the photo that was shown to me by one officer, another officer asked me, "where do you keep your porn?" I said, "I have lots of porn, but nothing illegal, I can assure you." I opened the closet and pulled out boxes of DVDs and VHS tapes. (many years earlier I took care of AIDS patients and many of them during that time when AIDS was new, in the 1980s, some parents put their children out of the home. These people had no one to visit them or any contact with anyone, due to the hysteria surrounding this new plague.) God sent me to visit them. Some old and some new friends and take them ice cream and whatever I could. Trust me, I'm not 'Mr.

Goody Two Shoes' by any stretch of the imagination, but we all basically know what's right, and some of us act on it and some of us don't. I, for some reason, am able to put myself in their shoes; I would also hope that someone would come to bring me ice cream if it were me. It's just that simple. (or do unto others as you would have them do unto you). Uncomplicated! try it.

To this day I go to nursing homes to visit old jazz musicians, and artists taking them ice cream, grapes, etc., and just sit. I fondly remember sitting with one of my nearest and dearest friends, Ruth Ellington, sister of one of America's greatest composers, Duke Ellington. She was old and dying and had fallen apart. The vibrant woman I spent such wonderful times with was so happy that I came to hold her hand and try to make her smile, and the great singer Dakota Staton, one of the finest singers ever, and never made a dime. Not really. For all her talent, only small money and even smaller fame… how sad. Listen to her for yourself and hear sheer brilliance. I'd sit with her in the nursing home, and many times I didn't think she even knew it, blind, and bedridden; but I remember once I kissed her on her head as I was leaving, after sitting for a while, and she said, thank you JaRon.

The same exact thing happens when I was sitting with the wonderful swinging Jazz organist Sarah McLawler in the nursing home; and after sitting and talking and rubbing her hand, I kissed her forehead and said, 'sleep well my friend', and she whispered thank you JaRon. I understand now that they may not have words to say, but they are aware of us. A few floors up in the same nursing home, was one of the great dancers and choreographers ever, ‚His work is too numerous to list here. (I was so honored to have met him through our mutual friend and my business partner in Parlor Jazz, Mary Cannon Screen. We call her FiFi).

Mr. Louis Johnson resides, I stop in often and bring him Cheetos and sherbet, and he's so happy. We sit and watch TV and it doesn't matter if it's anything fancy. These wonderful souls have given so much to so many, it means a lot when people stop by to visit.

These people have had a life in the public for 50 years, and now they are shut away in one room with a TV blaring. GO VISIT friends! It gives them oxygen, it's food for their spirit, also it's good. It's just part of my DNA. Many people up in age and alone get calls from me just to check on them, and say I love you. It's good for one's soul.

It's funny, but I never thought about it until now, writing this book, but maybe that's why my life is so calm and perfect and peaceful. (I could use money) of course, but all of my needs are met. things always work out for me because my center is right. We get back what we put out in the universe. God knows. And that's the truth, Ruth!

So now back to how I acquired the porn collection in the first place, forgive me. (I sometimes go on a writing journey because there are so many thoughts in my head, but I always make it back to the real nitty-gritty and finish the thought. It may take a minute, but exhale and relax. Anyway, these young men many suffering from AIDS and some women died over time. Many were struggling to make ends meet, as most are then and now, and had no money, so a few left me the few pitiful possessions they had, mostly their porn. I have had an entrepreneurial spirit since I could walk (I got it from my father). So, when I got the porn (all legal) I thought I could eventually sell it to a porn store. I'm kind of a hoarder in a way, which I call an archivist because I really do save everything, never knowing when I may need something. My world is so spontaneous, I simply must be prepared. For example, here is a scenario for you to ponder, and this really is how my life operates… worldwide on many continents. For instance, I'm walking down the street, pick a street, anyone, in any country, and I pass a shoe store, or a candy store, or a porn store, and the owner says he has had enough, to me, a total stranger,

He continues, I'm leaving the business, why don't you take it over? Now in the back of my theatrical mind, I said well, l at least will have porn already to sell. Yes, I know I'm nuts. but that's how my life works, it's my DNA. Like Billie Holiday sang, "everything happens to me, listen to me".

So, in one of the boxes was a disk with 12 photoshop pictures of pre-teens, (not real photos mind you, or real preteens, but photoshopped almost cartoons like over-exaggerated body parts, etc., which no one would take seriously. I surely didn't.

But what they did not find was real child pornography, none, nothing. Not one video of real children. They also did not find any searches for that material on my computers, (it's just not my thing) no real photos at all, nothing to do with real child porn.

There was also a disk of a TV show on the same station that my Jazz TV show airs, MNN in NYC, which is where I taped it from dealing with a district attorney in NYC, who was accused of child molestation and it aired right before my TV show. It was pretty explicit on public access tv. That's all that was in my home. And let me be clear. I have no intention to re-debate re-litigate this case, just tell the story.

So, here is another piece to this puzzle I'm still trying to decipher, as you may be, as you read this. I went through it firsthand and I'm still not clear to this day. This is therapeutic and cathartic for me to tell this to the world. Someone, perhaps, who has been through this will be helped by my story.

My old desktop many years earlier crashed, and the apple store said to back up everything often just in case you have a crash, you will have a backup of everything, So I would just copy stuff to disk all the time, just in case. Once I got a strange email link, I clicked it and porn after porn after porn kept coming up on my screen, all kinds of stuff and it wouldn't stop, every time I clicked something, it took me to another porn site, so I had to unplug everything. When I copied stuff from the computer, those 12 cartoons like photoshopped pictures were part of the other stuff I copied,

For maybe 35 years I have copied 1000s of tv shows, most of the old Hollywood movies, of the 1930s- 40s- 50s- and 60s, many Johnny Carson shows, Burns and Allen, and every jazz show and singer that has been on TV since VHS was invented, I would record it. I'm an archivist and I just keep and save stuff.

My closet is full, from top to bottom of that stuff. So, when they saw my collection, they thought they had a major child pornographer. Just the sheer volume of DVDs, VHS, I assume they thought they had the largest porn bust in history. When in reality, they found nothing.

People who are into that scene, won't have 1 disk in their home, but 1000s upon thousands of links, searches, DVDs, nowadays I'm told flash drives, which I didn't even know what that was in 2009.

So many people have no idea how police officers lie. The ones who came into my home were all white. I had coffee with a dear friend and wonderful pianist Lucy Gallagher recently. As it turned out, she and I had a big gig out near the Hamptons the time I was arrested July 4th weekend 2009. And also, as it turns out, she happened to be on the grand jury on my case, which I didn't know there was a grand jury.

She told me over coffee, that the police told the grand jury that they found 1000s of child porn in my home. So, help me, God. And it was

The Nightmare Starts

an outright lie. But one thing I do know, God will surely make it right.

But let me take you back 6 months before the police came, when this all started. Being a jazz musician, I always need money; and from time to time, people would visit NYC and sleep in my spare room 'for a few days only' and 'contribute' shall we say to the cause.

One such person came to see the room and I decided it wasn't a good idea since I can tell within 10 seconds whether I'm going to get along with someone or not. He left and later the next day we were talking on AOL chat, and the conversation got heated and he said to me, "I'm gonna get you and you are going to lose that apartment". I blocked him after that and wondered aloud what a strange comment. But paid it no more mind.

I went to bed and when I awoke, my internet had been shut off. I was sure I had paid the bill, so I called AOL and I was told that my account was closed and there was nothing they could do. I was instructed to write the AOL corporate office. I wrote to them asking why my internet is shut off; they would only say there's nothing they can do. I was assigned two case numbers, 137 69 3318 and 137 722 749 (this was early winter 2008 I think)

What recourse does one have when the company says you're suspended. I couldn't fight it, but I found it very strange. I had been using a free signal for months prior to getting AOL reconnected, my internet was off for many months because I couldn't pay the bill. When one has no funds, you make do with what you have. A free signal allowed me to get online.

After my account was closed on AOL, I had to move on. That was the start of my life changing existence.

Shortly before my internet was shut off, when I was still using a free WIFI signal picked up in the air, it was no neighbors living next to me or below me or over me. They were doing renovations; I was told that anyone versed in computers can stand right in one's hallway and go right into an unsecured computer. This person who went by the email likeswine @ ... was the one who made the threat, saying ' I'm going to get you and you are going to lose that apartment', and I believe deep in my soul this is how the child porn video the police were looking for was sent out. It didn't, however, come from me. Of this I'm certain. To this day I'm computer dense. And this was 2009. And besides, I couldn't look at such a video. To harm any innocent life is just wrong, but a child is beyond the beyond.

Also, a new friend in Brooklyn, named William J, who is an internet wiz with a thriving company looked into it, and he came up with the name William P. out of NJ who used that email and made the treat. So, in my mind, the video could only have come from him. He looked like I had seen him in the area before, near where my landlord lived at 216 East 85 St., where I lived for 25 years, right down the street from where I live now at 222East 85th.

I lived at 216 East 85th St for 25 years. For 10 years I was the only tenant in the bldg. The landlord had gotten everyone else out. Some, according to the New York Times were poisoned. Old Germans, since this was Germantown. These people were so racist and nasty, they flooded the apartment above mine, so my ceiling fell in; and they put holes in the walls and the building was full of rats; they shut off the heat; they sent goons to run me out. It was a nightmare. The only tenant for 10 years. and I went through hell. My original landlord, Steven Stribula, the father of the landlord now was brutally murdered right next store to my apartment and turns out the man who murdered him, a Mr. Murphy, lived in the building where I live today. But I don't scare. Like Marvin Gaye said, *"Let's Get It On.*

The Nightmare Starts

Once the landlord realized I wasn't going anywhere, he had to buy me out and put me where I am now, with the same lease from 1972. He took me to court so many times I lost count. The first offer was 50,000 Dollars, I said to him that wouldn't get my clothes out of the cleaners. I think I had 75 cents to my name. (but 'you gotta know when to hold em and know when to fold em') Thank you Kenny Rogers. He asked me how much I would take to move. I said give me $250.000 and I'll leave tomorrow. He my landlord Joseph Stribula said I'll never give you that. So, I said, "fine, I'll stay put." He couldn't renovate the building with me there, so I was holding up progress. But I was not going to lose my home in the middle of Manhattan.

So, my wonderful Lawyer, Alan Goldberg, got me everything I wanted, which was the same rent stabilized lease and $15,000 and a new apartment.

Now, in reading this book thus far, you've read earlier how my landlord, Joseph Stribula (the son of the first landlord) and his family have fought me for close to 35 years to get me out of my lovely 5-room apartment, where I have the same lease since 1972, a 5-minute walk to the Metropolitan Museum on New York's chic Upper East Side. Unless one is a New Yorker, none of this makes any sense.

Well, after 35 years of dragging me through court to get me out of my apartment, (starting with his father many years earlier) he had one last chance to remove me before selling the buildings he owned and leaving the city. He owns many many buildings and is worth a king's ransom.

It was a Black Hispanic couple (Eddie and Beatrice who cleaned and scrubbed and fetched, picked up trash and generally took care of the buildings. Although they were darker in skin tone then I am, you couldn't tell them they weren't white. Sad. Anyway, everything I did, they would run and tell the white landowner. The landlord would cough, and they would ask, 'we sick boss?'.

I had Eddie come over to fix the bathroom pipe, and he saw that I had painted my apartment walls a color other than white, and he ran as fast as his legs could carry him to tell the landlord. Now, again, we had been fighting for 35 years. (think Hatfields and McCoys). He's very wealthy, so going to court for him was part of what landlords do, I guess. I, on the other hand, can't rub two quarters together, and couldn't afford all of the court costs; however, you may remember somewhere in this book I mentioned, earlier that I'm blessed? And highly favored? Well, it's true. God blessed me with the, or one of the, best housing Lawyers in NYC, Alan Goldberg, and his law firm, on East 45th Street, off Fifth Ave. I could never afford him, but this Jewish angel, this kind and wonderful and tough as nails lawyer fought my case (for whatever money I could pay) on and off for 35 years. I can only explain or believe that God had to be in charge. *Can you explain it?* This wonderful little man fought my case and kept me in my lovely home on New York's Upper East Side. I pray for him and his family often. The world needs more Alan Goldbergs.

So, after the building super, Eddie, ran and tattled to my landlord, Joseph Stribula, the landlord sent me a letter saying he's taking me back to court for eviction if the walls are not painted white this week.

After over 30 years of fighting, I had enough and wrote him a letter, which is printed in its entirety for you to read. Now I have to admit that it's a very strongly worded letter, which is to be expected from me when my back is against the wall. But I will understand some of the readers to be highly upset with it. But, we all make choices.

The Letter

Joseph Stribula/Herma Stribula
JAS Management
216 East 85th St, Suite 1A   3/9/2009
New York, NY 10028

I am in receipt of your newest scribe insisting that I change the color of my dining room to white. It's a pity that you choose to spend your summer in petty squabbles such as the colors which bring me peace and tranquility in my home. One would think that after the vicious and brutal stabbing death of your father the original landlord of this property, and the equally sadistic and vile murder of your older brother, and even a third murder, that of your sister's husband, after all of that profound destruction, reasonable people would learn perhaps a modicum of decency and humility for life and liberty.

I guess the adage 'the apple doesn't fall far from the tree' rings true in your family; so perhaps that's asking a little too much.

Since you have blown the bugle and chosen to wallow in the mud over this non-issue, I have gone to my battle station and I'm preparing for all-out war in court against this silliness. And make no mistake about it, I plan to go to the Supreme Court, if necessary.

It's a shame that such a young man in the prime of his life has nothing better to do. Now I'm forced to get in the mud with you. However, in the meantime as long as I'm living here, I shall be comfortable in my surroundings. When and if I leave my home after living here for 35 years, I'll be more than happy to paint the walls any color you like.

I can only pray for you and your family, the sadness in the faces of your mother and sister pains me. May God have mercy on you and yours. But to quote the bible 'One reaps what they sow' Perhaps one day in this life, or the next, all of you can find happiness.

I have contacted my lawyer and forwarded your letter to him. I thank you for your patience, understanding, and consideration in this matter.

Sincerely

This was hardball; and shortly after this letter, I was in jail, framed. I deeply believe by a white racist wealthy landlord who was selling the property (I was told it was sold for about 10 million) and this was his last chance to get what he considered my 'uppity Black ass' out of his properties, of which he has many, for good.

However, I don't care how big, how rich, how white, how important you think you are, I'm sitting on God's shoulders, and I guess you didn't hear, 'yo arms too short to box with God' (1976 play by Vinnette Carol.)

But years earlier, I dated a wealthy white woman, you may recall earlier in the book, and after one of our disagreements, she said to me 'be very careful, people like me can harm you and you will never know it'. Only I strongly believe it was the landlord this time. For people who don't live in NYC, let me explain what many people living here considered.

Rent stabilized apartments are considered the gold standard of apartment living. I'll spare you, the reader, the laborious details of just what rent-stabilized apartments or rent-controlled is. But the short version, it's an apartment/ home which may rent for $5,000 a month normal rent, and someone with a stabilized apartment may pay $500instead. So, it's very coveted, I have to keep referring to earlier in this book when I told the story of my apartment. I had no idea I would be framed for a crime, just to get my apartment, and I'm not going to go back to the early part of the book and rewrite it; so, you will have to bear with me and just re-read it, cause I'm trying to tie it all together, and it's a lot. So, smoke a joint, legal and (medicinal of course) and relax and go on this journey with me.

Here are just a few marquee names who have had or have a rent control/stabilized apt in NYC.

Congressman Charlie Rangel (more than one) a legend of the halls of power in Washington, the wonderful actress, mother of the great investigative reporter, Rowan Farrow (yes he does look like 'Old Blue Eyes') and ex-wife of legendary Hollywood director, Woody Allen, Mia Farrow. She had an 11-room apartment on CPW, one of the most expensive areas in the country, so did the Ex-Governor David Paterson - he had one in the same building as Rangel.

The great writer of 'When Harry Met Sally', Nora Ephron, Mick Jagger's Ex-wife Bianca, had one on Park Ave. Cindy Lauper, a wonderful talent, the great actress, Faye Dunaway, had a small rent-stabilized apartment near me on the Upper East Side, and she was sued to move out. All of the famous people, at one time, had or still have what I have, a rent-stabilized apartment, with cheap rent, in one of the most expensive cities on earth.

Some of these people were forced to give up their homes. However, they have the funds to live anywhere. Even so, who can pass on a deal like this?? And it's legal. In my case, I had to fight to the death to keep my home. I wasn't leaving, otherwise, I would be homeless today.

You can google how so many landlords in NYC do whatever they could to evict tenants from their homes to charge market rent. It's all about greed. From poison to murder. It's legendary, there are 8 million stories in the naked city, this is mine. Even the rich can't resist this deal

Now, many of you who don't have this deal or see it as just wrong to pay cheap rent, don't get upset at us, or me. Don't take it out on the tenants, it's the LAW.

Now back to the police in my home. The officers surrounded me, asking me questions about my being in a major child porn ring and producing videos worldwide. They made me write a confession saying that I was such a person. I wrote that I had never sent out child porn and was not involved in anything remotely close to a nationwide ring However, when I was reading my paperwork from the case almost two years later, while still fighting it, and when I had the strength and mindset to finally go through the papers, I was shocked. The judge had been giving a supposed signed confession where I admitted to being in a nationwide child porn ring, (an outright lie).

The police took me out of my home in handcuffs, on a bright summer day, still early morning. I, who have never been in real trouble in my life, now in my middle 50s facing the most horrific ordeal imaginable. I will never forget the landlord's face. He was standing on his steps, watching me with a smirk on his face, full of glee. Probably saying to himself, 'I got that uppity N---- now'. I'm sure he was very proud of himself. Probably slept really well that night, knowing he had won after over 30 years of fighting me. (But like Arnold said, 'I'll be Back.' I was put in the back of the patrol car and my mind slowly ran amuck.

We got to the precinct and I sat in a room with several officers trying to get me to admit stuff that I wouldn't, because it was not true. I had never cried so much in my life. the kinda crying where you heave, lose one's breath, and snot and drool, and just a mess. You really cannot imagine, unless you have been there. After hours of questioning, I was taken to a cell called central booking or something, where we have to wait to see a judge. I was in this cell with lots of people and again trying to hold on to what little sanity I had left, when this well-dressed black gentlemen came to me in the holding cell and singled me out. He looked into my eyes and said, this is your first time in jail? I said yes. He said you are here for a sex crime, am I right? I said yes. He said, "Take my card, I will help you." I was sure God had sent him.

After several hours, which seemed an eternity, I was taken before the judge and not knowing what to do or what to say or anything, I was like a fish on land.

I was told by the judge that my bail was $50,000. In New York, it's Not 10%. It was $50,000. I couldn't reach anyone because it was the 4th of July holiday and most people were away, and nobody knew where I was. I finally reached my dear friend and business partner Norbert Bogner and told him where I was and why I was there. He called my Sister, but because it was the holiday, my family couldn't reach any bondsman to start the paperwork, and they didn't know what to do in New Jersey and I was in NYC. But, at least, they knew where I was and why I was there. I was told by my brother-in-law that when my sister heard why I was in jail, she lost her mind also, as did my mother and family and friends worldwide. It was just unreal. a sordid dream from a Hitchcock film.

After a few days in holding, they shipped me off to Rikers Island (a Zoo) mostly because of the guards. but more about them later. In fact, all about them. After a week, my family found all the necessary players and paperwork in this drama; and my wonderful mother put the family home up as collateral. You see, the plan was for me not to make bail and they were already set to send me upstate for 10 years. The fix was in. I believe my landlord did his job well. When you spread enough money around, you can make shit happen.

I was housed in a big barn-like place with about 100 mostly young and wild drug dealers, gang members, violent predators, murderers, rapists, and some innocent as I was, simply caught up in a racist corrupt system. I had never seen such a display of characters replete with folly. It was loud 25 hours a day, literally screaming at each other across the room when one is in bed A and one is in bed Z, and they have a conversation all night. Stunning. I called my dear friend Linda one day from the jail phones, whom as you remember we met at jazz pianist Barry Harris' workshop in the early 80s, and she was with me when I got sober at the Sarah Vaughn show, Bluenote New Year's Eve 1985. She told me later after I got out, that she was never so concerned or upset, just hearing the background noise on the phone; to this day she can't forget it.

I found a small bible on the floor next to a table. I picked it up and clung to it. I read it all day and all night; I still do. It's next to me now, 10 years later. I will keep it until the day I'm dead. Because you can't bring anything into jail, I had nothing except the clothes on my back.

A white guy who was in a bed next to mine had 2-3 pairs of dollar store glasses, (I'm not sure how he got them or if he had been there a while and had them sent to him. That's the place you go to while waiting to be sentenced.) He was kind enough to give me a pair.

It saved me, for I couldn't read anything without them. I wish I knew who he is so I can hug him and say thank you.

I prayed all day every day, one prayer. God, please do not let me lose my temper, for if I do, I would kill somebody, or somebody will kill me. Most likely the guards would have, because my temper, once unleashed, is 'no return'. The young gangstas would gather next to and around my bed and talk shit to each other all night and try to engage me.

I would pull the sheet over my head and lay in the same position for 12 straight hours never moving. Once a guy touched my head and I leapt out of bed and they jumped back. I looked at them and went back under my sheet. Because I was snorting heroin in the 60s, and 70s, it would make you go into what's called a nod. and you could maintain the position for hours. usually standing and nodding down toward the sidewalk. I just did it in the bed because that's where I was. It was a form of meditation, just zoning out.

So, I channeled myself to that nod to avoid any contact with the other inmates. Once I went to take a shower and I got naked as most people do who take showers, and they screamed at me, PUT YOUR UNDERWEAR ON. I had no idea it was a prison rule to always keep on your shorts in the shower. Now how in the hell am I supposed to know that? There should be a guidebook on the rules and etiquette of jail life.

I was clueless about everything. You see when I was in Jack and Jill in the 1960s, I didn't read that in *Emily Post.* Nowadays, I pray that I can work with the prison department to help first time people, because I went through hell, and nobody tells you anything. You just have to figure it out and make mistakes along the way, hoping to survive daily fighting, gang wars, just total madness. It was simply unreal.

It took almost 2 weeks to get the paperwork once the 4th of July holiday was over and workers were back to work to prepare my release. For a musician or most artists, 50,000 dollars bond might as well be 50 million.

My first time in trouble, and I had no criminal history, and a 50,000-dollar bond was set. I believe, knowing I had no funds to make bail; and that way if you can't make bail, the state owns your ass. So many poor people are in jail, as you read this, simply because they have no funds to make bail…another form of modern slavery.

I would love to see rich sports professionals, entertainers, and businesspeople who many of these inmates look up to, start a fund for first timers and helping them through this trap. Surely, the money I make from any and all the things I do, will start a fund. It may exist now, and I don't know about it. It's just so sad what goes on in America. But God is watching all.

Remember, when I was in Berlin Germany and my mother had a stroke? The family put her in a nursing home and had planned to sell the house. Well, I saw it differently, so I came home to get her out of that place and put her back in her own large beautiful home. She was able to live by herself for several months, I think; then the family put our mother in an assisted living home which was wonderful, with her

The Nightmare Starts

own furniture, and surroundings. So that was, I agreed, suitable since she had another stroke and it wasn't wise to be in the house alone.

Well, think of this. if I had not come home to get my mother out of the nursing home, I wouldn't have had the family home as collateral to get the $50,000 to get out of jail. *You see how God works in my life?* So, after 2 weeks on Rikers, I made it out alive but then the real nightmare began.

I couldn't wait to contact that lawyer, Arnold P Keith, who found me in the holding cell and offered to help me. I felt I would just waltz into court in one of my expensive silk tailored suits and have my lawyer explain this foolishness, this huge mistake, and all would be right with the world. My lawyer went over the case and agreed to take my case for $10,000. I have to, once again, thank my God; because of friends, I raised the money in 48 hours.

My friend from the late 70s, Miss J from the show, *'America's Top Model*, sent me $1,000. Ms. Alma Carroll in Brooklyn NY, a dear friend who founded the Jazz Consortium, who was lso the wife of the wonderful swinging Joe Carroll, sent me $1000. Another dear friend for many years, Marva, sent $2000. My cousin in Maryland, Dr. Ed. sent $2000, and a few others sent the balance needed. I'm grateful. I paid back what I could over time. But the love was there. I don't think I have had to ever ask for money in my life. So, everybody was shocked, I guess. I met with Mr. Keith and we started going over the case and almost from the beginning, I had my doubts; there was something about him that wasn't authentic. But I was so sure God had sent him to me while I was losing my mind in a cage.

I told him how the police changed my statement, where I had written down that I had never been involved in child porn; yet when it got to the judge it had been changed that I *had* been involved. I explained to him that I was never read my Miranda Rights, and he showed me paperwork with a signature saying to me, "sure you did, here is the document."

I said, "look at that signature, it's not mine." So, he said, "oh you're right, but its ok". More and more of this happened; but I had never been in trouble before, and he was a lawyer. What did I know? I just went along with him, until I ended up in Rikers Island.

He was the most incompetent and or corrupt lawyer I had witnessed, but then he was the first criminal defense lawyer I ever dealt with.

The original judge in my case was Rena Uviller. You may recall reading earlier about a one-time love in my life, I called her D (A lovely French lady), years ago. Well, she happened to be the court Stenographer for this judge for over 20 years and wrote a wonderful letter on my behalf, which dozens of other prominent people did, and I don't believe my lawyer ever showed them to the judge. There were so many things this man did to sabotage me. It was shocking in hindsight; but as it was going on I didn't fully understand it until after the fact.

I trusted him and he sold me up the river. Whatever the racist young white overzealous prosecutor, Mr. Kevin Wilson wanted, he got. I firmly believe that no white man with my background would have gone to jail for this crime. It was sad to see this white man, in my opinion, walk over Mr. Keith. It was as though he was intimidated by the white prosecutor and a little out of place. At one point, Mr. Keith said to me, "I'm glad you hired me because most would have hired a white lawyer". When I met this man, I was so happy and grateful that God had sent him to me to save my life. I thought I was hiring Johnny Cochran; but instead, I got Amos and Andy wrapped into one sad fool.

At one point, the judge admonished my lawyer for being ill-prepared or something close to it. and basically, told him to get his act together before he's back in her court. I won't go into the ins and outs of this case and just cut to the chase. I begged my lawyer to go to trial, that this was a lie and that I believed that my landlord was behind this to get my home… and it fell on deaf ears. He and his partners at the law firm, Hornstein, Palumbo and Keith, despite my pleading, said to me, "either take the offer of 6 months in Rikers Island jail or you will go upstate to prison for 10 years. I said, "It's a lie, 10 years for dozens of photoshopped pictures? Has everybody gone mad?" I'm sympathetic to Jimmy Hoffa's case when Robert Kennedy went after him overzealously. But that was political. This was personal. At least, I'm still here and standing. After this book is published, if anything should happen to me or I end up in a similar state, you know where to start looking.

I couldn't imagine going to prison for 10 years, the mere thought sent me into madness. Hell, six months in Rikers was just as bad for me. But I'm certain I wouldn't have come home from that.

But what could I do? I fought my case for two years out on bail and was free to do as I pleased until that day of reckoning,

The lawyers kept saying it's my only hope. I didn't know at that time if my landlord had maybe paid them all or just my lawyer and he had convinced them to just send this one up the river and I owe you a favor. Remember, this lawyer found me in a holding cell and came over to me.

According to the American Bar Association (Rule 7.3 solicitation of a client), that's illegal. So, I'm thinking someone paid him to be there to find me and represent me for the desired outcome. I don't want to be paranoid, but you have to admit that it's a bit strange.

I talked to other lawyers after the fact and all said I shouldn't have ever gone to jail for this weak case and with no real criminal history; and that my lawyer was incompetent. They obviously had no case because they went from 10 years to six months.

I'm sure he will rue the day that he dismissed me. I told him it was a lie, and he gave me to the white devils. Hornstein, Palumbo, and Keith (whom I call Curly, Larry, and Mo.) all agreed that I take this plea… and so I did.

I was scheduled to turn myself in January 2011. I had a feeling of complete numbness that morning, getting myself-ready, leaving my wonderful home, full of love and God. I spent Christmas with my family in Baton Rouge, Louisiana and enjoyed being with my mother in her failing health.

That cold morning, I made my way to the courthouse and the judge said to me how do I plead? And I said, "guilty." My lawyer said to me when the judge asks you, say nothing except guilty, and he stressed it. I prayed I had told the judge how my lawyer was incompetent and or corrupt, but it was the furthest thing from my mind at that time.

I had a signed letter from the judge to be placed in protective custody due to the nature of the case and my 56 years of age. Immediately after the sentencing of 6 months, I was handcuffed and taken away like a common criminal and placed in a cage. My training in Jack and Jill certainly didn't cover this.

We were all lined up like cattle in chains, wrist to wrist. The gentleman (and I use the term loosely) behind me that I was chained to, as we were herded into a waiting van, said to me, "the first N---- who looks at me, I'm gonna bite his eyes out." Well…Where does one go from there? One of my good friends, Vince G, had been in and out of jail for years and happened to be out as I was going in, LOL *It sounds so weird to even say that.* Anyway, he said to me, ``the first thing you get there is a Walkman for the company.'' Once I got settled, I did. Someone was leaving as I was coming in and gave me his. We made our way to Rikers Island and this drama was live and in living color.

I couldn't possibly write every detail of prison life, but I'll share moments for the sake of authenticity. Once you get to Rikers, you are packed into cages, 20- 30 guys, all sleeping on concrete floors. Guards screaming at everybody, inmates screaming at each other, Complete insanity… fights, augments and just loudness… 25 hours a day, 8 days a week. For a person such as myself who spends hours upon hours in the solitude of my lovely home, this was beyond torture.

It takes maybe 24-36- 48 hours before you are assigned a bed, and until then you slept on the concrete floors caged like wild animals in chains. They do give everybody a medical test and other tests, which is really a good thing for people without any other means. I finally got to my temporary bed, caged in this small room underground with only a few inches of window peeking above the ground.

This was my first night, after maybe 2-3 days in bed. I had my Walkman and was laying in this tiny filthy dungeon contemplating my life and the world I live in. I must say from time to time, this was truly a nightmare for me and only people who know me personally will really get this, but others who read this will also, of course, understand from a different perspective.

My Life was flashing before me, at the same time I'm living it. I thought of all my world travels, and interesting people I have met and talked with and dined with and lived with and sexed with and enjoyed with and laughed with, was all before me as I lay in a dungeon for a silly lie. I was listening to the genius that is Jascha Heifetz, performing most brilliantly a Brahms Violin Concerto. It brought tears to my eyes and joy to my soul. Complete bliss and tranquility, despite my surroundings…until I noticed movement on the little metal stand next to the bed about 3 feet from me.

Upon a closer look, I saw it was a RAT. I jumped out of the steal bunk and asked the guard to come at once. I said to him, "there's a rat in here", and he said to me, after a pregnant pause, that 'the rat was here before I got here, and will be here after I'm gone", and not to fuck with him again. I had expected him to either remove me or the rat. I understand that I'm new at this shit, and unaccustomed to all of it, but realized that one doesn't ask for shit in jail.

Then it sunk in that I was on another planet and I had to adapt to a new world until I was out of it. A few days later, I was moved to the protective custody where the judge placed it.

It wasn't so bad; I had my own small cage. Private, and the best thing was there were only maybe 8 people on this floor.. What a blessing, I was sure I could do my bid and survive this. I was safe, reasonably comfortable, quiet; and I could just stay in my cage and pray, think, and contemplate. I asked my friend Norbert to send me books, so I got a lot of reading done and made notes about this book, which I knew I would write. On this floor was a black cop who had gone rogue, an Italian wannabe mobster I called 'Johnny two toes', some Arab terrorist wannabe, a black drug dealer, 2 other nutjobs, and me.

I felt okay about it, I had friends put money in my account to buy food from the commissary, since jail food is worse than the worst food imaginable; and I'm a gourmet chef, so that was a real adjustment. We didn't have to leave this space for anything, all the food came to our floor where we ate in the TV room; so, I felt good to just stay in my section and read and write, away from the madness. The white guards in this building were nice. I was called Mr. Eames and respected. We all would meet in the eating /TV room to hang out during dinner. It was a small and sane gathering; except for 'Johnny two toes' who tried to get into my business while I was cleaning the bathroom. He came into the room trying to tell me how to clean, and remember I prayed to God daily to just let me keep my temper; otherwise I would be killed, or I would kill somebody.

But I had to back 'two toes' down and he came to realize that although this was my first time incarcerated 'this ain't my first time at the rodeo' As Mommy Dearest said, "after that, I had no more issues and felt good about serving this time and moving on. The judge who sentenced me in my case was Kirke Bartley, the very same judge who sentenced Anthony D, Marshal to prison for swindling his socialite mom. What a sad and troubling end to the legendary grand dame Brooks Astor of the Astors. Norbert had sent me more books and I was doing my time and praying to just get out, and grateful that I was safe.

One day I was in my small cage and the phone at the guard's desk rang. I heard the guard speaking and asking, are you sure? He asked that same question again a few times, "are you sure, Mr. Eames?" Then I heard him say, "Mr. Eames, pack up." I asked, "where am I going, to Paris?" I had gotten that comfortable in jail, where my personality was not completely dead. He answered, ``You are going to the general population…GP…"

I said, "that's not possible, I have a signed letter from the judge that I'm to be housed here." He said, "yes, I know, but I was just ordered to have you move now. Let's go." I passed out. All of the life left my body, I was being thrown into the belly of the beast. I felt my soul completely leave my body. I had convulsions, foam came out of my nose, eyes, ears and every orifice in one's own body. I was lifeless, dazed, zombie-like. After a short while, I made myself-get up off the floor and put my few pitiful possessions into a plastic bag and marched with a guard into general population with guys, many of who are career criminals of the worst sort. They would just kill you as much as look at you. Rikers Island has to be one of the worst prisons/ jails in America. It's Notorious.

All of my years of my running the streets and getting in and out of situations worldwide came into play. I ran with dope dealers, to killers, since the 1960s. This was the ultimate test of character. My mother asked me once after my high school graduation in 1971, 'don't you have any decent friends? Are all your friends dope dealers and other characters?' Unbeknownst to me, despite being the banker's son, all those years of street-running helped me survive Rikers island. That's no place for the weak. I walked into a dorm with 60 beds and inmates, Mostly Bloods or Crips. When you walk in, everybody in the dorm is looking at you, and if you show any fear they will eat you alive. And it's no help.

I went from a Clark Gable/Billy Eckstein persona in my entertainment world to Charlie Manson persona in this zoo. I had never witnessed anything so vile, vulgar, vicissitude of fortune. I walked in like a madman. A full white beard, big silver bushy hair, dentures out, and looking like Fredrick Douglass. Completely ready to kill or be killed. I had to keep a perpetual snarl on my face for my entire stay in this nightmare. I had to squat an imaginary fly off of me to keep the demons away. I talked incoherently and mumbled as though I was not all there. I never made eye contact, unless necessary. I never talked, unless necessary, trying harder than you can imagine not to lose my mind, and to just be. A most strange existence for someone with my sensibilities.

The Nightmare Starts

I found an empty bed and crashed down, exhausted. Remembering how I used to count the NINA's in Hershfield drawings. Little did I know or realize that there are so many prison rules, protocols, do's and don'ts, although I never read about it in Amy Vanderbilt writings. Certain beds are for certain people; don't ask me who they are but I couldn't get just any bed.

It's amazing the strange things like these thoughts that went through my mind as part of the bigger picture to help keep me sane. I would lay in bed and pray to God every second, 'dear God, please don't let me lose my temper, dear God, please don't let me go off in this zoo because I know that I would be killed, or I would kill somebody. I prayed this all day, every day. But it finally dawned on me, this was the plan all alone. After dealing with me for 35 years, my landlord knows my temper better than most. Hell, he's seen me in action. what better way for him to have me removed than to have me in jail and killed in a fight by an inmate or guard?

Remember, I had a court order from the judge, which my incompetent lawyer, Arnold Keith, could not or would not enforce to get me back in Protective Custody. He allowed Rikers to move me against the wishes of the judge; then lied to my friends and family telling me everything was okay and he's getting me back in PC. He never did and he also allowed Rikers to hold any money that friends and family put into my commissary to buy food while in jail, so I was fucked, and my incompetent lawyer was responsible for it.

Oh, the guards also told the inmates that I was a child abuser. I'm in a dorm with 60 mostly cutthroat gangstas and the guards tell them lies about why I'm in there, which was meant to have my face slashed as a gang mark. Some guys would walk around my bed and take their thumbs and run it from the corner of the lip to the ear, which is how they wanted to slash me. I read my bible all day and all night.

Most of the fights and other problems started while marching in a long line of maybe several hundred prisoners going to chow. One line was on one side of the wall and one on the other side going the other way.

Now, if one of these young idiots looked at someone the wrong way, shit hit the fan, and my old ass was caught in the middle. A nightmare indeed. Jail is a place where 5 am, an army of mostly Black and Latino guards will come into the dorm and get everybody on the floor, and toss all of your few nothings and fruit which we keep to snack on into the trash, make you strip naked and bend over and cough, and just fuck with people because they can. Mostly black and brown people.

How sad is that? That you chose a profession, which your sole purpose is to make people's lives miserable. What a shame. White people have trained many blacks officers to do their dirty work. It's a way of transferring the self-hatred. The Black guards were worse on Black inmates than the Klan, it was so disheartening; and I'm sure they will have a million reasons why they have to do it, but it comes down to self-hate. After all we have been through in this country, and you would treat your brother like this is the essence of meritorious manumission in play, Live in techno color.

All the TV talking heads rant about Black on Black crime, which is mostly young Black knuckleheads fighting each other over foolishness most times, and shooting each other, which is so sad, but it's nothing new.

It's strange you never heard the same talking heads talk about white on white crime, when Frank Costello Meyer Lansky, Charles Luciano were shooting each other. In December 1985 I was riding my bike and almost witnessed the murder of Big Pauli (Paul

Castellano) who was hit by the mob. I saw his body on the sidewalk of East 46th St. and 3rd Ave.

The female guards were worse than the male guards. It was as though they hated their Black fathers, brothers, husbands, sons, and grandsons. It was so sad to see Black people treat each other in this manner, I'm so unaccustomed to that brainwashed mindset. Once many of the inmates were all sitting in the TV room watching the game, and they started asking all the guys 'what hood are you from? So, they all said the name of the hood they came from, Bed Stuyvesant, Red Hook, Brownsville, Gun Hill Road, and on and on, so it got to me and I said, the Upper East Side, neighbors to the Kennedys, Rockefellers, Vanderbilts, so they all stopped and looked at me like I was completely mad and said, that Negro crazy, and changed the subject. Thank God. You can't lie there; they know every hood and each other.

Many of the guards were worse than the inmates. Once a white guard took me into a closet and got in my face and said Eames why are you always causing trouble? Now I never did or said anything, so I knew this was a set up for a beating. I have never been so scared in my life. I saw other guards around before he took me into the closet. A bell sounded and he had to leave. Thank God. I swallowed my heart.

After maybe 6 weeks in general population, I was very close to losing my mind completely, to the point of no return. I was a basket-case. Sleeping with one eye open, loud screaming, fighting, lights on all night, I can't say it enough, *it was truly maddening.* Wondering 24 hours a day which one will cut my face, or if I was forced into a situation, certainly I would be killed, or I would kill. This is a categorical fact. To live like that was more than I could bare. One night I was having a heartfelt conversation with the guy next to me in his bunk, Sha is his name, and I was telling him about my life on the outside world, and how I ended up in the Twilight Zone. Part of my breakdown was due to the fact that my landlord sent me a registered letter almost daily saying that he was going to put my stuff on the streets, and I would be homeless.

I was going on and on and, reminiscing, and trying to remember who I really am, and the life I have led and all the fabulous dinner parties with socialites, in penthouses worldwide, and activism work I've done, and the book I had written, etc. and performing in Europe and Asia and and… and…Then he said to me, "that don't mean shit in here, you are just another jailed negro." I said to him, "I can't take another day, I'm about to lose it." He said, "you will have to take it, bro. but if any shit goes down in here, if any of these young knuckleheads make a move, I know mother fuckers that got yo back, the oldtimers in here like the way you carry yourself, you won't have any problems." Then he turned over and went to sleep. He was an old player, been in and out, and knew the ropes. I was really in a bad way. More than I can say here.

The persona I had created for Rikers was so convincing. I had given the 'Greatest Performance of my Life' as my Music Idol Nancy Wilson who just passed December 13th, 2018 would sing.'But if you had been behind the curtain when it fell, you would have seen this actor crying'. I simply couldn't keep this up. I was ready to snap. I'm certain I would have met death, or I would have killed someone, and it was approaching fast. And I knew it.

For almost 3 months I had been living in an alternate reality. Kinda like 'Kelly Ann Conway'. I found myself hovering over my body, looking at me. I was trying to make sense of it and could not believe I was there in prison.

I once again slept with one eye open and praying 'tonight is not the night I would kill or be killed'. I can't tell you how hard I prayed. That next morning, I didn't go to breakfast, why bother, just cold slop with many awful people. By that time, my spirit had left my body, only a shell was left.

I kept a partial dairy while in jail, knowing if I ever got out I would tell this story. I wrote many names down in the bible that I found on the floor near a table and read daily in Rikers to help carry me through this nightmare/reality show. Today, I still have that same bible where I scribbled the names of many of the guards I dealt with while in Rikers. Over time (it's been years) the ink has faded in the bible where I wrote them, so I apologize that I can't say thank you for what you did for me. I think of you fondly and often. Bless you, my angel.

There was a beautiful black female guard whose name I no longer remember, and I owe her my life. This beautiful black woman came to me and said are you okay? I said 'no, I can't take another day here'. I can't'. I had never thought of suicide ever in my life, but if I could've taken my life I deeply think I would've.But for the fact, my mother would lose her mind. And family and friends worldwide. But I was desperately close.

This angel who asked me if I was okay, said, "you are coming with me:. She got me up and we walked to the Psych Ward. The Dr. looked at me, asked me a question, and before I could answer I collapsed onto the floor. All the mental anguish and torment I had been carrying inside me since being in prison came to a head when I got to the mental ward. If I had broken down in the population, it would have been over for me. Once you show any weakness or fear, it's over. And for the last 3 months I simply couldn't keep it up. In other words, when you have to live 25 hours a day 8 days a week as a persona, after a while it and you will crumble. I crumbled.

Shortly thereafter, 3 guards from the general population floor where I had been for 6 weeks, came to get me to bring me back. (One was the guard who took me into the closet) You see they hadn't finished the plan to destroy, disfigure or kill me in this hell hole. The guards got into a heated discussion about them bringing me back to the dorm. However, and unbeknownst to me, the Psych Dr. has the last word. I heard him say, to the guards, 'this man cannot go back upstairs, he will stay here in the Psych ward'.

I thank God. You see, once I was in the psych ward, I was safe. Rather safer. It was the nut wing, only about 20 people or so, in a closed environment. You didn't have to leave this dorm at all, the food came to this ward. It was much safer, because everybody was on psych meds, think *'One Flew Over the Cuckoo's Nest'*. (a great Jack Nicholson film - 1975). It was the deepest sleep I had in prison. That night, I went out from months of no sleep. Because all the inmates in this dorm were a bit nuts, and medicated. It was relatively calm.

After a good sleep, the Dr called me into a meeting with a group of big shot doctors. After evaluating me, all agreed that I could not go back to the general population, but that I would have to take psych meds in order to stay in this ward. That was one of the worst things I have ever heard. I'm someone who at 65 years old now takes no pharmaceuticals at all, I just do not trust most of them However, I'm now taking a blood pressure pill and I'm not happy about it. Every now and then I take an aspirin, but I'm grateful to be healthy where I don't need any meds. But now I'm told I have a choice, take psych meds or I would have to go back to the belly of the beast to a tragic end. My brain was soaring into orbit, thinking over and over and hearing loud voices in my head saying, 'if you take psych meds, your personality would die, and that quality that makes you, you, are dead.

Or the other choice was to go back to general population and face unbearable torture, of mind body and soul. I would have my face cut up and worst.

Can you imagine? Hobson's choice? What would you do? Well, I often say that I'm blessed, and have always been. I'm grateful. The Doctors said to me, "Mr. Eames, what will it be?" I said, "due to my religion I can't take any medication." They said, "what do you mean?" I said, "I'm a Christian Scientist."

Just for the record, I am not now, nor have I ever been a Christian Scientist. But a dear friend of mine is a Christian Scientist, Mary Ellen, and I would go with her to her church on 77th and Park Ave, here in NYC. So, I was familiar with the doctrine; and thank God, being open to other ideas elevates one's mine and can at times save lives…as it was in my case.

The doctors had no idea what the hell I was talking about and asked me to go back to my bunk and they would call for me after lunch. Well they did their research and when I was called back to this Pow Wow I was told 'Ok Mr. Eames, you can stay here in the mental ward and won't have to take meds. You see, Christian Science is a religion where prayer works best without taking medicine.

Thank God,

Once again, were it not for that beautiful Black woman who saw her brother in deep pain and took me away from the madness, brought me to safety; and the Psych Doctors who allowed me to stay without taking medicine, this could've turned out much differently.

I settled into my new home for the last month of my stay. It was winding down.

When I woke up, for the first time since being locked up I had some semblance of hope. I still had another month in Rikers, and in a place like that, a month is forever. It was maybe 20 guys in this mental ward, all lined up like good little soldiers following orders and waiting for the Dr. to give them pills to take, then they would proceed to walk around most of the day in a fog. I'm sure some needed it, but the bright light that I have always possessed since birth and before would have been dimmed permanently. And that, my friends, would have been a shame. I have much more to give.

I remember that the food was so bad, just awful. It really was as the old-timers say 'slop'. But when one is hungry, you eat just to stay alive, as I did. Oh, I think every Thursday we had baked chicken. Tasteless, but with a little salt and pepper when we could get it, it was edible. Every now and then the guys serving the inmates would make the second round of baked chicken, and we the inmates would line up with our hands extended for them to put it in our hands and we would walk away, sit, or stand and enjoy this treat. One is always hungry in prison. The little things like a banana, or just anything to eat was so special. I dreamed of food, day and night. Seafood Gumbo, Louisiana Poboys, Hagan Daz chocolate ice cream, Oreo cookies, and on and on and on. It helped to keep me sane.

The main thing I loved about being in the mental ward, was safety. All the food came to us and we didn't have to leave and go to mess hall where all hell could break loose any second. My dear friend, Norbert, sent me books and I got lots of reading done. After a week or so, the head Dr. asked me to come into his office. So, I get there, and he says to me "Mr. Eames, I just wanted to thank you." I said, "thank me for what?" He said, "so many of the inmates speak so highly of you for taking the time to help them with problems."

For example, there was a big strong guy in this dorm, and I asked him about his family, and he said Mother's Day is coming up and to be sure to contact his mom. He was perhaps late 20s and was going on and on about how he hated his parents and hadn't talked to them in over a year. They didn't care about him, etc. That sent me into a mild shock not speaking to his mother for over a year and yet I spoke with my mother almost daily from anywhere I found myself in the world, since I moved to NYC in 1972. But I had to realize that many didn't have the upbringing I did and that deep family love. I'm sure talking to one's mother daily is a bit much for most. Lol That kinda love will carry one through the most difficult times imaginable. It did for me.

He started saying how they hated him, and he wouldn't care if they never spoke to him again. He said he didn't even have a phone number for them. So, I said, "look this is your mother and father, at least let them know where you are and that you are okay. I'm sure they are worried to death of your whereabouts.. And if you don't hear anything from them, then perhaps it's time to move on." I wasn't aware that this young man could not write or read much. So, I wrote out the letter, very simple, saying '*hi Mom- Dad, all is okay; however, I'm in jail at Rikers Island for another few months*. I wanted to say Happy Mother's Day'. But that sounded like me, so I said, "take from this and put it in your words from you."

Well, in less than a week he received a letter from his parents, they sent him their phone number and he called. He cried, they cried and had a nice talk, and shared as only family can. That gave me great joy. There were a few instances like that. It made me feel almost human again.

It was my dear friend Carolyn McClaire, one of the leading publicists in the Jazz world and assistant to the legendary founder of the original Jazz Festival - 'Newport', Mr. George Wein. My dear friend Carolyn would make a three-way call, once I called her so I could talk to my mother.

I'm sure if I had not had that, nothing would have saved me from going mad, killing someone and never getting out of jail. My time was winding down now and I started to see a bit clearer. I was going home soon. However, I deeply believe that my being in jail hastened the death of my mother, and for that I'm inconsolable. I have nightmares and I rage in private. Those, who I believe had a hand in putting me in jail for a lie, have put a hatred in my soul that I pray one day to exit from my body.. But it's hard, and it brings up years of injustice that I must speak about now.

Unless you have been in a cage, you can never know the feeling of being let out of a cage. I was released from Rikers Island after serving in total four months. That can be life for those of us who have never been incarcerated. I spent that last Christmas 2010 with my mother and brother Kirk and his wife Rita, in their home in Baton Rouge, Louisiana. We had a great Christmas dinner and Rita is a great cook. But It was so difficult to enjoy Xmas knowing that in a matter of weeks I had to report to the courthouse in Manhattan and taken right to Rikers.

I went into Rikers in Mid-January and was out Mid-May 2011.

When I walked outside of jail it was the first time I had seen or felt the sun, smelled the air, feeling a shell of myself, but at least I was alive. I left whatever I had come with, which was very little. They gave me bus fare to the city. I had let Norbert know to contact my dear friend Mary Ellen to leave my house keys with her doorman.

She lives in one of those midtown buildings on Madison Avenue and many of the homes in that building sell for many many millions. Now, I had just gotten out of a cage and *looked* like I had just gotten out of a cage. I made it to Manhattan and proceeded to make my way to the East 60s and Madison Ave to get my keys from the doorman. I walked in looking like a jailbird, dark circles under my eyes, jail footwear, clothes I found in the trash in Rikers. FYI-(All of my dress suits are hand-stitched with the finest thread and fabric by a master tailor in Thailand). I waltzed in and went to the concierge, standing in the lobby looking like something the cat dragged in; and in my best Sydney Poitier voice said, "I'm Mr. Eames and there's a package for me, I'm here to pick it up."

He looked at me like I had two heads, with a pregnant pause worthy of an Oscar, then gave me the package. I thanked him, and like Fraiser, 'left the building'. Walking up Madison Avenue to my home on East 85th off of Third Ave, I had tears in my eyes the entire way. Remember, part of my nervous breakdown in Rikers was due to the fact that my evil demonic landlord had sent me registered letters 2-3 times a week threatening to put all of my possessions onto the street. So, I had no idea if I had a home to go to, or if he had changed the locks, or hell for all I know he could have burned the building down, just to spite me. The hatred was just that deep, all 30 years of it.)

I got to my building walked up the 5 steps leading to the front door, put the key into the lock, turned it, with tears in my eyes, not knowing what to expect. *Would I be homeless?* The door did not open. I could have swallowed my heart, it felt like it was coming out of my chest. In my nervousness, I had turned the key the wrong way. I turned it the correct way and it opened. I walked in, walked to the second floor, and prayed that he had not put a padlock on the door or changed my lock.

I put in the key and opened the door to my home. I collapsed onto the floor and sobbed for what seemed like hours. *I was home. I was home.* My heart goes out to Central Park 5.

Part of the after-effects from my breakdown in Rikers was when I got out I would have severe crying spells… I mean major crying and convulsing; it would start, and I couldn't stop it. I was diagnosed with severe PTSD. I had to stay home often, due to my crumbling and sobbing on buses and trains. It was like I was living in another place, another time. And If I think too long about what happened to me, even today, I go into a very dark place and relive every moment. Then I go into fits of rage. I have always had a bad temper, but after Rikers, it's a time bomb.

'There is no place like home' took on a different meaning. I called my mother and said I'm home. She cried and we talked. I told her I was safe and just needed a bath, food, and sleep, and I would call her tomorrow. My wonderful family paid the bills while I was in prison. The next call I made was to my shyster lawyer, Arnold P. Keith; he answered the phone, and said, "JaRon??" I said, "I'm out." He said, 'how did you survive?" I found that response deeply telling, coming from my lawyer, who I deeply believe did everything he could against me. Why would someone ask that unless they were expecting me not to survive? Umm. *If you didn't know me…* I perhaps could understand it from someone else.

I simply said, "God," and I hung up. (George Carlin one of my heroes, would hate that statement; he would understand though because it's not used in a hypercritical way.).Anyway, I just saw my lawyer, Arnold Keith, July 2019 for the first time since my release in 2011, sitting in my Doctor's office on East 79th St off Third Ave. He didn't see me, he was texting with his head down, and I walked in to pick up what I needed and left. I didn't want any contact or interaction with him or to spook him before this book comes out.

It took all I could do to keep from confronting him. I can't remember a time I have had such deep hatred and violent thoughts for anyone. That's why I blame him, and everyone connected to this case with the death or my mother. Her baby in a cage for a vile lie; it tore her heart apart. But I take comfort knowing that she knew it was a lie.

After those two phone calls, I drew myself the hottest and deepest bath with bubbles, and oils and scents, and Epson salts. I took a container of the best Seafood Gumbo out of the freezer and slowly defrosted it, as I soaked four months of filth off of me. I had not had ice for four months, and I had a bucket of ice next to the tub, for ice-cold water. I lay in the tub listening to Sarah Vaughn, with candles and incense burning. I was home. My mother at the age of 88 had a massive stroke in 2011, and because I was on probation for 10 years for having only a few underage photoshopped pictures, I was not allowed to go home to see my mother. It took a few months before the lawyer I hired, Matt Myers, (one of the best in the city) could arrange for me to go home to see my dying mother. I went home and she was in a bad way in a nursing home. I lost precious months dealing with silly rules before I could get to my dying mother.

I had so little money, then and now. But all of my needs are met! Always.

I drove home and went straight to Ollie Steele Nursing Home in Baton Rouge, Louisiana. I got to hug my best friend and the best mother on earth. I sang to her, I wheeled her out in the sun, and danced for her, made her smile, as hard as it was due to the massive stroke. I would read my book to her, and rub her face saying, "you are the best mother;" and I told her how much I loved her. After a week of this, on my last visit, I took her back to her room. They had to use a machine to get her into bed. I kissed her on the mouth as we always did, and I said, 'I'm okay, I handle it. Let go now and be with daddy." She went into a fetal position; and I rubbed her wonderful face and left the room.

I got a call from my sister-in-law, shortly after I left the home saying, 'Cookie has passed'. I was relieved. It was unbearable to watch my mother suffer. I prayed for her to go ASAP. I had thoughts of helping her in her transition, rather than to watch this marvelous woman in the state she was in.

Now it pains me to say this, but it must be said. Probation had kept me from seeing my dying mother because of some foolish rule that a fool made. (Any fool can make a rule, and only another fool will follow it) 'Thoreau'. To keep a son from his dying mother is sheer insanity.

Think about this. There are people who are not allowed to see a dying parent because of rules and regulations that are heartless and inhumane and medieval. You will never get the chance to kiss your mother, hug her, say goodbye to her.

I'm certain I would have taken a gun into the office of probation and killed those who kept me from my dying mother. (I really hate to write this, I hate to even think about it, but I know it's true; for me, this is surely what I would have done). Then perhaps the rules may be changed.

Sometimes common sense has to take charge in these matters, workers cannot let a piece of paper dictate humanness. Of course, I don't suggest people do what I would have done, but please don't play with people's emotions when it's something as important and final as death.

The Nightmare Starts

Probation was almost worse than prison. Having to report everything you do 25 hours a day, 8 days a week.

It was unbearable. They come to your home, look around, ask silly questions, it was truly maddening. You have to go to the probation office once a week, and they make it known that they have the power to make you come daily if they so choose. The first year I felt I was still in prison due to the very strict and almost childish rules they put grown people through. And some of the probation officers were in lockstep with this foolishness. However, I have to admit that the people in probation (H. Bridgewater, D. Moore, and L. Levern) over time started to treat me as a real person, not just a number/ criminal. Then slowly, I started to get my life back, I believe that probation realized I wasn't the monster the paperwork said I am. I told them that it was a lie. It's always the truth and then there are the facts. But they deal with hundreds of criminals daily for years, so why would I just automatically expect them to see me for me. Most of their contact is with the great unlettered and unwashed. I'm grateful for their help. It took time, but they all came, it seemed, to change that hard and strict policy they put me through.. I had to follow the rules, no matter how absurd. I had to acquiesce daily. (Where ignorance is bliss, is folly to be wise.)

Some of the people who dealt with me were very kind and over time, years actually we developed a real relationship. If you truly want to know what a person is made of, just give 'em power. Some use that power for good, unfortunately, many don't..

The attorney, Matt Myer's office had a wonderful young lawyer, Jason Richland, who got me off probation in October 2016, after five years. I'm deeply grateful for him. I did a musical tribute to Nancy Wilson to celebrate her 80th birthday at the Sugar Bar, the night before I went before the judge to be released from probation, and I sang a song of Nancy's (her first Grammy win in 1964), *How Glad I am*. I meant it. After 35 years of no drugs and alcohol I felt I needed Marijuana again to keep me sane, and I started smoking the day I got off probation, (for medicinal purposes only, of course.)

Nothing in my life has been as difficult as being falsely charged with a crime and put in jail.

Yet it's happened to more people of color on a daily basis. You read in the paper and watch news programs where men (most seem to be overwhelmingly Black) have served 10, 20, 30 years for a crime they didn't commit; and this is due mostly to white racist police officers who literally outright lie in order to get a conviction, and a white racist system with the power to destroy lives.

I pray for the day when good White police officers stand up for what they know are right and help their department get rid of that certain destructive energy, which is on every police station in the country. That simple act would go a long way in restoring the trust Black people have in White cops. Because, as of now, there are none. When we can't call the police to come when they are needed, the Black person who calls could be shot dead. And that's a sad reality.

You hung Black men and castrated them, hung Black women and if pregnant cut opens the belly and ripped the child out and killed it. You burned Black people alive on crosses, denied basic human rights, schools, education, housing, police brutality This history needs to be faced so we can all move past it. Some of this madness was happening in my lifetime in the Jim Crow south. That's recent American 1960s history. Perhaps we need to start teaching real history in all schools. It's sad to say it's a consistent hatred, centuries of it. Where does it come from? Has this ever been asked? Why is this taught to white children, year after year, all these years? I don't think white people will ever have real peace until this question is faced head-on. And, until white people realize that centuries of severe white hate and racism are the cause of the Black condition today around the world. We all need a lot of prayer and healing. What the power structure doesn't want is people who are capable of critical thinking.

What must be in the hearts of the Caucasians who possess that DNA, which is hell-bent on the destruction of Black and brown people for centuries? It's been said that this particular type of Caucasian is so afraid of Black people coming into real power because they feel that Black people will treat White people as inhumanely as White people have treated Black people for four hundred years. News flash: We won't. It's not in our DNA, we don't have a history of that in America. That's *your* history. To simply be left alone to our own devices, would be true heaven. Try it. But I'm deeply afraid of where I see the country today. White cops killing Black men on Television (I can't breathe). Black boys shot dead for having toy water pistols. Brown children thrown into cages after being snatched away from their mothers and fathers. (in 2019) You know the headlines, no need to list them all here; but America is at a breaking point now. We are at a major crossroad; something is about to explode in the country and it's a fight between good and evil. I deeply believe good will win. It usually does. The old guard white mindset is fighting tooth and nail to hold onto the last vestiges of power. Not to see this through rose-colored glasses, but to quote Rodney King, "Can we all just get along?"' It pains and saddens me to say it could be major disruption on the streets of every city, nook and cranny in the USA, and it brings to mind Baldwin's *The Fire Next Time*. I'm merely asking why not try everything we can to save this country before it gets to that point.

I am of the mindset of self-segregation, meaning, blacks have to get land and start our own society and country inside of a country. The definition of insanity is doing the same thing over and over and expecting different results. Caucasians' power-structure, after 400 years, has made it abundantly clear; they cannot live in peace with Black people, so why do we keep pretending we can. This is nothing new, Elijah Muhammad promoted this in the Black Muslim movement in the 1960s and before, and Marcus Garvey long before that. The majority of both races want to live in peace and harmony, of that I'm certain; but that element with deep roots in white supremacy is getting deeper, although the minority. And I thank God for that.

However, the backlash to President Obama is being felt daily. I get so upset (no that's an overstatement, I get mildly amused) with Black movie stars, and musicians, etc. who constantly complain and gripe every year.

The Oscars, or the Emmys, or the Tony's or Grammys, or this, that or the other don't have any blacks represented. Well, why do you care? Why don't Blacks start their own Oscars? Grammy? After all these years, you still expect white people to treat you as an equal and fair? It won't happen, or rather it hasn't happened in centuries, so why do you keep running behind the power-structure with your hand out. In a just and fair world, we are citizens and entitled to what all Americans are entitled to. But don't hold your breath. Now is the time in history for people of color to circle the wagons for survival. There are many decent white people, but the white dominant power structure is so ingrained in every aspect of our lives. I'm not sure it can really change, so it's only reasonable to have your own shit. Period.

Everybody is tired of the same topics, day after day, month after month, year after year, decade after decade, generation after generation, century after century. So, maybe, just maybe, it's time to

The Nightmare Starts

try something very radical. In fact, make the Black Oscars so wonderful and magnificent and glorious, and grand, and delightful and delectable, and (well you get my point) that the entire world would be in long lines to get in. Kinda like when James Brown came to the Apollo Theater in 1962. The lines were around the block for blocks. But we must not forget on May 31, 1921, in Tulsa Oklahoma, the wealthy Black business district known as the 'Black Wall Street' was so successful, jealous racist white mobs were infuriated that Blacks were doing so well in most cases and they decided to massacre hundreds of Blacks and burn down the town. It was one of the many sad chapters in this country's history. So yes, it can be done, and it has been done, but white rage is real and that reaction to Black success could be done again. Be prepared.

Many of my dearest friends and close acquaintances are Caucasians. Norbert is my brother. (from another mother) And some of the most wonderful soul's that God has put breath in, I'm grateful to call them friends. And those wonderful people and many like-minded people are the majority of white people and not like the ones which cause hell for others. Friends won't always agree, so I find it best to avoid most politics. We share so many other wonderful qualities we can share. It's very difficult to have a real discussion about race in this country, most whites feel attacked or harbor deep guilt, but I believe it's a defense mechanism. But whites need to ask each other: *why, after centuries, is this deep hate still there?* Personally, I'd love to see every major Black sports figure shut down sports, period. Now, half of America just went into an uproar. What, no sports? Yes, it's time to try any and everything to save a bloodbath in America.

No more running up and down the field, throwing balls for wealthy white owners until these same white owners call every police station and politician and say enough, get rid of the racists in the department, now. *Black Lives Matter*. They can do just that because money is a major part of this structure I'm talking about. It's a multi-Billion-dollar industry. But the Black athletes would never do that. So, it's a moot point. They are not sick and tired of being sick and tired, they need to channel Fanny Lou. I do salute Colin Kaepernick. "Unless you stand for something, you will fall for anything". Athletes from days gone by, like my hero Ali, Jim Brown, Olympic winners Tommy Smith and John Carlos who raised a fist to protest injustice, Bill Russel, Jesse Owens, and so many more, all took a stand. It's not just about being paid millions of dollars today and ending up soulless.

The great Bob Law, (one of my mentors) would always say, he couldn't understand why wealthy Blacks can't wait to move to all-white neighborhoods, where they are not welcomed or wanted. Then he would say, "why don't you build your neighborhood and make it so special that whites can't wait to get in?" For me, it's the only way I know. It's how I was raised. That's what I did with my Parlor Jazz @ Home. I made it so special that all people can't wait to get in and I don't have to run behind clubs to hire me.

Norbert in his wisdom says I can really sing Sinatra's (Paul Anka wrote it) "My Way" because I've lived it. With all the Black money in America, it's shameful that there are so few Black-owned Jazz Clubs. Or Black-owned radio stations where you hear our real culture, not the mess, which people who don't look like us and are hell-bent on promoting. Black destruction and genocide are the real agenda. You ever ask yourself why you never hear a Jewish rapper saying horrible things about Jewish women or Italian rappers never say negative things about their women, etc. But, it seems to be okay when a small but loud Black gangsta rap genre call their women every derogatory name that they know and talk about drive-by shootings and sadly killing innocent children or anybody, with frequency. And that's what played worldwide. Again, I believe it's a part of a systematic plan to demonize Black youth so they can continue to build more prisons.

I'd love to see if Ari on MSNBC would give as much time on his hit TV show to a white Rapper who called their sister and mother out of her name. Just asking.

Since I'm mentioning TV stations, I'll share this story with you about CNN's Don Lemon. We were at an event, and I said to him "Mr. Lemon, I'm JaRon Eames, and we are both from Louisiana, etc. and I told him that I had written an important book on Black American Jazz called, *Historical Jazz Conversations.* It should be in every HBCU, and music school, and I'd love to have it mentioned on CNN. Would you have any ideas for me? He looked at me and said, " I only do big stories." He turned and walked away. I guess he never heard of each one, teach one, and reach one. We as a Black race need a lot of healing, and prayer.

My being an old Hollywood trivia guy, I first thought of Norma Desmond who Gloria Swanson played so brilliantly, in the great Billy Wilder film of 1950, *Sunset Boulevard,* when Gillis, the young writer played by William Holden said to her, "You used to be big;" and she said, "I'm still big, it's the picture that got small."

Anyway. The white power structure says Blacks should pull themselves up by their bootstraps, but when we do white rage takes over. White rage is real and what's to say it won't happen again? Remember Tulsa? Well, it happened also in the East St. Louis Massacre of 1917, when racist white mobs attacked successful Blacks and kill hundreds and burned down the town.

Unless we remember and learn from the past, who is to say it won't be repeated? The climate is ripe for it, as I write this. Everybody is on edge. It saddens me to say this, but justice denied is a lightning rod for riots. This government has enough arms to destroy the world. So, a war against the power structure is a fool's reality. However, when people of color are killed by the system and nobody is held accountable I'm concerned of hand to hand combat on every street, on every bus, train, restaurants, movie theaters, highways, parks, and Disneyland. It brings tears to my eyes to have to think this way; but if you have a better solution, please share it. NOW. People are at their wit's end. You cannot force people to live together, it has not worked in 400 years. Now the hatred has boiled over. So, why not try self-segregation? Many whites don't want to live with Blacks; so again, my suggestion is since this is a big country, we get land where those evil whites are not around and build a community of unity and love and peace. Hell, they built Vegas in the desert. Surely we can build what's needed to survive …including an army.

I'm sure this sounds over the top for many; but many have accepted a life of racism and hatred. If the races can't live together, (we have had centuries of trying) then separate. Or we spend an eternity in a fog, pretending. 'Oh, oh oh, yes, I'm the great pretender, pretending that I'm doing well'.) It was a major hit for the Platters in 1955. I tell you what, let's build a land where whites, Blacks, and others who want to share and live and love and learn and laugh and pray and grow together. Really get to know each other for real, not just surface bull shit. A place where it's truly Utopia. It is my deep belief that whites and Blacks, really do love each other, despite all the madness we hear and see daily. Deep down, it's a love-hate relationship. Kinda like an old marriage. Can't live together and can't live apart. Now, that truly is mad. (maybe that's why I'm single.) But it has worked all this time up to a point. That would be ideal. But we have to want it and make it happen. Now is the time, we need to shit or get off the toilet.

Then, we put all the Evil racist whites and stupid Black loud gang bangers and other groups of idiots and troublemakers, on their own land. Give them knives, guns, ice picks, bats, chains, brass knuckles, to fight, and hate and kill each other at will for all time. So, the rest of us can all live in peace. And enjoy sidewalk cafes, wearing something cool, and listening to Ella sing "These Foolish Things," while having a cold libation. I started to travel again, all over like I used to. I'd visit friends in Europe. I stayed at my dear friend Rosie's quaint villa on the Mediterranean Sea where I walked barefoot and exhaled. I visited Tallon in Paris, or Margrit in Berlin, and friends in Switzerland. (of course, I had no funds, but that's never stopped me before). However, my light was returning.

I started to feel like me in earnest. My soul was back, the good energy I have always had was here again. My Hollywood smile had returned, my eyes had a glow. It had all been lost while in a cage. (can you imagine, demons tried hard to put out my light, they came dangerously close.) My dear friend in Youngstown OH,. Alberta N. sent me a card while I was in Rikers. On the front of the card was a forest, lots of green trees and strong branches. But one tree was wilted and bent over. The caption said, you are like this tree, and you are still standing because you have deep roots. I did and I do. And I thank God every second of every day for my deep roots. The ancestors watched over me, including the ones in my past life. Shirley McClaine would understand.

In fact, I told my brother Marvin, when I got out of prison, that he should buy a pair of sunshades. He asked why? I said, "in time, my light will be so bright, you will need sunglasses just to look at me."

One of the first things I did after getting out of the cage was to clean out my home. I wanted to remove everything in it that subsequently reminded me of that morning in 2009, when the devils came, took me out in handcuffs, and left Satan's energy. So, I repainted my living room a brilliant red, to compliment the Waterford chandelier, painted my piano room a soft blue, and my small foyer an even softer gold. I have looked everywhere for my own entertainment space to wine and dine and sing and perform for appreciative people who remember old school Black entertainment. I wanted a night club in NYC. All of my life. Instead, I have a 'Day Club" JaRon's Parlor Jazz, in my home on Sundays. Norbert is the maître d and Fifi is the host. Nothing brings me more joy and satisfaction. On many Sundays, 20-30-40 people come to my home where they can hear one of the most wonderful pianists in this business, Ms. Emme Kemp, who co-wrote Bubbling Brown Sugar 1976 on Broadway. I have book readings and enlightening conversations. I had to go to hell to get this inner peace that I have now. Money can't buy it. Because of my deep connection to God, I believe this is His will for me and it's my divine birthright. As the wise sage, Paramahansa Yogananda says in the Law of Success, "I want success without measure, not from earthly sources, but from God's all possessing, all-powerful, all-bountiful hands."

An Atheist may not relate to this or those who just don't deal with or have any relationship to God. But for me, I had to surrender. God wanted my attention, the only way to get it was to put me in a cage. As awful as that sounds, and I'm sure you have heard people on the news who spent time, real time, in jail and after getting out says, "it was the best thing that ever happened to me."

Well, I must say I really do understand that statement and for years I would ridicule it. But I'm a believer in one having to go to hell to appreciate heaven. Some people just stay in limbo. Either, or. (people like that make me nervous.) As Oscar Wilde said, "The only thing worse than being talked about is not being talked about." I've always been extreme. I go all in. Like Chris Hayes. Of course, I don't recommend going to jail, but again I had to.

If one uses his or her time in adversity well, the outcome can be life-changing. I'm in the best place imaginable mentally, spiritually, emotionally, I'm a work in progress.

I'm grateful. Let the church folk say, "Amen!"

Stay tune for Act 4.

About the Author

Eames siblings at Erin's wedding (2018)

JaRon was born in Baton Rouge La, December 21st, 1953 to the kind of prominent family that W.E.B. DuBois publicized in his essays, 'The Talented Tenth'.

After graduating high school in 1971 and one year of college at Southern University, in 1972 he moved to NYC to follow his dream of becoming an entertainer.

About the Author

He worked for Japan Airlines on fifth Avenue in NYC from 1973 1977 and after traveling many places around the world he left the airlines to devote his life to Jazz. JaRon has been performing on stages for over 35 years. He is the host, producer of the longest running weekly Jazz TV show in History preserving and archiving many of the authentic legends of Jazz. (The JaRon Eames Show). On his show the masters of this music genre can tell their stories uncensored. He is currently at work on a documentary called Historical Jazz Conversations based on years of priceless footage from his television program.

His book is called: 'TAINTED'. A most shocking truthful story of sex, corruption, drugs, alcohol betrayal, racism, rampant incompetence, prison, vestiges of McCarthyism, and a corrupt judicial system run amok. But in the end gratitude, survival, redemption, surrendering, and real peace.

Acknowledgements

On September 23, 2019, I suffered a massive stroke. I spent 2 weeks at Lenox Hill Hospital and 2 weeks at Phelps. I am now home relearning to walk alone again. *It will take time.*

A Special thank you to Melissa and Emanuel and Dr. Avolio at Phelps Rehabilitation, to the Doctors and staff at Lenox Hill Hospital, and to the Fire Department on 85th St. NYC.

Thank you to my dear friend, Ms. Ellie (Kennedy) for all you do, and to Barbara Serlin for being there.

I also thank Louise Gross, Melba Joyce and Marylin Neilson, Jeanette Lasane, Gwin Black, and Emme Kemp for your encouragement, love and concern.

Thank you Bobby and Dhonna Goodale for your support.

Thank you to Everyone Who helped me on "Go Fund Me".

Also, My Special Thanks Go Out To:

Gina Reder, Doc. Al Vollmer, Local 802 Jazz Foundation, Joe Petrucelli. Will Glass. Melaney Mashburn, Victoria Horsford, Shahidah Shakoor, Wilma Jordan and Yvonne DuBose

Acknowledgements

Playwright Calvin A. Ramsey

Partners in the parlor - Norbert J. Bogner, Mary Cannon Screen, JaRon

Recordings

Suddenly (1994); Sounds Good to Me (1996); Caught in the Act, "Live" 2001, Romantic Classic -JaRon Eames sings, Emme Kemp Plays (2004) CD 2016 (Live in JaRon's Parlor and Live at the Downtown Club!)

Contact information:

JKE Productions, Ent. Inc.
Jazz/Blues vocalist- Author, Parlor Jazz
paypal.me/realJazz

222 East 85th St. Suite 2e
New York, NY
Phone/Fax 212-472-9295 or Cell 646-337-0620
JARONEAMES@Gmail.com
www.jaroneames. Com

www.ingramcontent.com/pod-product-compliance
Lightning Source LLC
Chambersburg PA
CBHW070547010526
44118CB00012B/1253